THE AUSTRALIAN
LEADERSHIP
READER

Six Leading Australians
and Their Stories

Edited By
Helen Sykes and Erica Frydenberg

Published by
AUSTRALIAN ACADEMIC PRESS
Brisbane

First published in 2006 by
Australian Academic Press
32 Jeays Street
Bowen Hills QLD 4006
Australia

ISBN 1 875378 66 9

Cover and text design by Andrea Rinarelli of Australian Academic Press, Brisbane.
Editing, and typesetting by Australian Academic Press, Brisbane.
www.australianacademicpress.com.au

Printed by Watson Ferguson & Company, Brisbane

CONTENTS

Preface

Over previous decades the editors have had the privilege of research-ing and working with many young people. As participant observers, we have listened to numerous interesting speakers of various ages, engaged in discussions with enthusiastic young people, and received many emails about their thoughts and feelings. It is these experi-ences, particularly the powerful influence of listening to peoples' stories, which has motivated this book.

What is the point of telling stories about six high-profile leaders? The leaders described in this book have shown a capacity to face up to difficult issues and a sense of perspective in challenging circum-stances. They have demonstrated that they can, in the public inter-est, stand firm against established views. These people exhibit leadership and influence in their pursuit of ideas and public debate about important societal issues. Their ability to cope with such responsibility sets them apart as inspiring role models.

This book is a collaborative work. The editors wish to thank the authors of the profiles and the leaders for their commitment and outstanding contribution to the project. We also acknowledge the generous contribution that Australian Academic Press has made to this publication and the constant support of our families.

All royalties from sales will go to the Trust for Young Australians to assist Indigenous young Australians with leadership opportunities.

About the Authors

Kylie Miller has worked for eight years at *The Age* in Melbourne, the past six as a television columnist, feature writer and deputy editor of the Green Guide. Her 16-year career has included a couple of years reporting for Canberra TV news bulletins, five years as a reporter at the Newcastle Herald, and a year on the foreign desk at the *Bangkok Post* in Thailand. Kylie won the NSW Young Journalist of the Year award in 1994 for a feature article on youth unemployment, which included a month-long placement at the *Straits Times* in Singapore.

Selina Samuels has an Arts/Law degree with honours in English, a University Medal from the University of NSW, and a PhD in literature from the University of London. She is the editor of four volumes on Australian writers for the *Dictionary of Literary Biography* and is Head of English at an independent girls' school in Sydney.

John Heard graduated with a Bachelor of Arts and a Bachelor of Laws cum laude from the University of Melbourne in 2005. He took the Supreme Court and Hearn Exhibitions for Jurisprudence, and an advanced legal research thesis he wrote on natural law won the Freehills Prize. He writes an online weblog as DREADNOUGHT and balances work in the corporate sector with an increasing output of articles and reviews. He made his first featured television appearance in January 2006

Lucinda Holdforth lives in Sydney and is a speechwriter. She has previously worked as a researcher at ABC television, career diplomat with the Australian Department of Foreign Affairs and Trade, speechwriter for Kim Beazley when he was Minister for Finance and Deputy Prime Minister, and communications specialist for a management consulting firm. She has had articles and columns published in Australian newspapers and magazines. Her first book, *True Pleasures: A Memoir of Women in Paris,* was published in 2004.

Felena Alach is a writer and visual artist who graduated with a Bachelor of Arts with first class honours in English from the University of Western Australia. Felena has worked for many recent years in the arts, and has written for various arts journals including *RealTime/OnScreen*, *Broadsheet*, *Artlink*, and *Photofile*, and is currently completing a Graduate Diploma in Internet Studies through Curtin University.

Larissa Behrendt is Professor of Law and Indigenous Studies and Director of Jumbunna Indigenous House of Learning at the University of Technology, Sydney. She is a practicing lawyer and lecturer and has worked with the United Nations. She sits on various tribunals and councils including the Administrative Decisions Tribunal and the University of Technology Sydney Council. She is widely published. *Home* is her first novel.

About the Editors

Dr Helen Sykes is the founder of Future Leaders (www.futureleaders.com.au), a national initiative designed to provide young people with inspiration and skill development for effective leadership and Going Further, a leadership program exploring the relationship between economic, environmental, social and cultural issues. Helen has conducted extensive research about young people and leadership and the attitudes of young people to the environment. She is editor and principal author of *Youth Homelessness: Courage and Hope* and co-editor of *Environment Education and Society in the Asia Pacific* and *Young People and the Environment*. Helen is president of the Trust for Young Australians, chair of the Royal Children's Hospital MHS Community Reference Group and member of the Australian Collaboration Steering Committee.

Dr Erica Frydenberg is a clinical, organisational, counselling and educational psychologist who has practiced extensively in the Australian educational setting before joining the staff of the University of Melbourne. She is an Associate Professor in psychology in the Faculty of Education where she is a member of the leadership and organisational learning cluster of academics. She is a Fellow of the Australian Psychological Society. She has authored 60 academic journal articles and chapters in the field of coping, published psychological instruments to measure coping, and developed programs and a CD-Rom to teach coping skills. Her most recent volumes are *Morton Deutsch: A Life and Legacy of Mediation and Conflict Resolution*, published by Australian Academic Press and *Thriving, Surviving or Going Under: Coping with Everyday Lives* published by Information Age Publishing in 2004. She has co-authored the *Schooling Issues Digest: Motivation and Engagement* which was published by DEST in 2005 and the Australian entry in the four-volume *Routledge Encyclopedia on Adolescence* that is scheduled for publication later in 2006.

Australian Honours Key

AC   Companion of the Order of Australia

AO   Officer of the Order of Australia

AM   Member of the Order of Australia

CVO   Commander of the Royal Victorian Order

CMG   Companion of the Order of St Michael and St George

How to use this Leadership Reader

This book is called a Leadership Reader because it does not try to define leadership, but instead presents a series of short essays about leaders to encourage the reader to fulfil that task themselves. To help the reader along the way the book begins with a brief overview of the very human trait of wanting to get ahead in life and how the concept of leadership involves issues such as personality, intelligence and coping. A series of questions about leadership is then provided as a framework for debate and exploration on each of the six leadership profiles that make up the bulk of the book. Five of the essays were written by talented young Australians who are already well on their way to future leadership roles in their respective fields. The sixth profile was written by the subject herself.

This book also provides readers with examples of non-fiction writing centred on contemporary Australian culture and recent history. Each leadership profile uses an individual writing style and approach to its subject. As you read the essays you will also be reading something about the author themselves, as their written voice inevitably weaves itself into the text and becomes an integral part of each story. The authors' impressive range of literary skills applied to the question of leadership include interviewing, personal reflection, descriptive prose, critical analysis, and informative narrative.

Lucinda Holdforth, a freelance writer, tackles the tale of a very a-stereotypical corporate CEO. Kylie Miller takes time out from her job as a journalist to seek the quintessence of a leading rock-star-cum-environmentalist. Felena Alach, an artist and freelance writer, embraces the challenge of exploring the life of an eminent, entrepre-neurial scientist. John Heard, talented law graduate and Blogger, delves into the values of an internationally respected Supreme Court Judge. A distinguished academic, award-winning author and signifi-cant Indigenous leader pens her own story. Selina Samuels, literary PhD holder, presents a very personal perspective on her respected statesman father.

Leadership

Getting Ahead in the World

We are all looking for inspiration — ways to enhance our performance across a range of activities. Often we come across people and events that inspire us by chance. We read self-help books or absorb the trials, tribulations, and successes of others in the hope that we will be encouraged and inspired. We can also learn from the world of research, where thousands of examples relating to a particular enquiry have been analysed and categorised to show us the common elements that lead to a particular outcome.

There are many concepts and issues that aid in our understanding of what helps people to get ahead in life. Concepts such as personality or temperament, along with ability and emotional intelligence, are considered to be predictors of success. There are many specific attributes and personal qualities, especially in the area of leadership, which are considered to be important aids to achievement. Additionally, the thoughts and cognitions that are associated with self-talk that individuals use to help or hinder their performance play a part. Sometimes these self-statements are conscious and overt, and at other times we engage them unconsciously. For example, in the world of tennis, leading players who frequently feature on our television screens often display their self-encouraging or self-deprecating statements when they congratulate or chide themselves over a stroke. Successful people often also have mentors who help them along the way, or role models who inspire them to pursue their passions and achieve their goals. How people cope with setbacks is also an important predictor of success in life.

Personality and Temperament

Both personality and temperament have a biological base, much of which is genetic. In contrast there are environmental characteristics such as a supportive family, school, or community setting, coupled with positive personality characteristics, which can make an individual resilient to adverse circumstances. Temperament is the foundation of what is later called personality. Temperament refers to observable, stable, individual characteristics of behavioural style. These characteristics, or dispositions, are present from early in life and are at least in part biologically driven and genetic in origin. They persist over time and across situations. For example, we know from studies that have followed young people from early childhood through to adulthood that infants who engage positively with the people and environment around them tend to remain socially well adapted through to adulthood. Nevertheless, what gives us hope is that we can develop desirable qualities such as ways of dealing with people that help us to get on with them. Additionally, we can learn to develop a positive mindset to help achieve goals and deal with setbacks.

Optimism is an important personality characteristic linked to success, achievement and leadership. It is clear that optimists do better in life in general than pessimists. Optimists expect good outcomes, pessimists expect bad outcomes. For example, optimists recover better from illnesses and surgery than do pessimists. As with all aspects of temperament and personality, research with twins show that such styles of dealing with the world are subject to genetic influences (Plomin, Scheier, Bergeman, Pederson, Nesselrode, & McClern, 1992). But optimism can also be learnt. Studies with adolescents and pre-adolescents indicate that when young people are shown how they can develop a positive way of explaining and interpreting the things that happen to them, they do.

Intelligence

Over and above studies of personality, which have been used to explain how we deal with life, there are multiple theories of intelligence. Since the first half of the 20th century we have considered an intelligence quotient (IQ) as measured by conventional intelligence tests as being an adequate predictor of an individual's potential for success. Over more recent years, there has been a challenge to the thinking that academic success, which is much of what is measured by traditional intelligence tests, is the best predictor of success in life. There are now several views of intelligence.

Howard Gardner, a renowned psychologist at Harvard University, writes about multiple intelligences, which according to Gardner are made up of at least eight types of intelligence, including spatial, musical, intra-personal, interpersonal, bodily-kinaesthetic, naturalistic, and the traditional academic. So there are many areas in which an individual can be successful. Another psychologist from Harvard, Robert Sternberg categorises intelligence into three types of mental abilities — analytic, creative, and practical intelligence (Sternberg, 1985). Finally, there are Salovey, Mayer and Goleman, who each write about the concept of emotional intelligence, which we will explore later. What is clear is that there are many different capacities over and above traditional academic intelligence that enable people to succeed in their endeavours.

It is now generally accepted that effective leaders possess multiple forms of intelligence. Gardner, in his book *Extraordinary Minds* (Gardner, 1997), presents portraits of exceptional individuals and examines their extraordinariness. The historically significant figures he describes are Mozart, Freud, Gandhi and Virginia Woolf. These four people possessed the capacity to learn from their experience and the capacity to frame and to reflect. They used their capacities and strengths to gain an advantage in pushing their particular fields forward. This he called *leverage*.

Like optimism and hope, Gardner described the capacity to construct experiences in a positive light as *framing*. That is not to ignore the reality or to negate failure, but to see the benefit that might be gained.

Reflect is a conscious attempt to pause and consider — to look both backwards and forwards. This can be done through the writing of journals, in reflective thinking, or in interactions with others. Reflection represents the capacity to draw on experience and to listen to others. This is not to discard one's goals and pursuits, but to consider what others are saying. It is the capacity to practice introspection, sometimes with the aid of a sounding board and other times without, a capacity to refrain from dwelling on weaknesses and to draw on one's strengths that enables the individual to move forward.

An additional quality that these people had was *passion* for their pursuits. They could focus on their activity without distraction from external stimuli. Others have called this capacity *flow*. Flow has been described as an effortless action that stands out as the best, such as an award-winning performance for an athlete or artist. Flow and *complexity* are regarded as sustaining talent and providing an "optimal experience" (Csikszentmihalyi, 1997). Flow is a subjective state that people report when they are completely involved in something to the point of total engrossment, where time may appear to stand still and the activity becomes all important, such as being engrossed in a novel, playing sport, or having an intense conversation (Csikszentmihalyi, Rathunde & Whalen, 1997). It is the depth of involvement that is intrinsically rewarding. Flow usually begins when a person takes on tasks or challenges just above his or her skill level. This leads to complexity, and the individual needs to find new challenges and perfect new skills in order to avoid anxiety. The duality between actor and action disappears. When one does what needs to be done without conscious effort this can distort their sense of time. The activity becomes autotelic — worth doing for its own sake.

In contrast to the subjective experience of flow, there is the quality of *perseverance*. This is where endurance or practice is required to achieve a stellar performance and the individual consciously strives to perfect a task or to reach a valued goal.

Additionally, Howard Gardner also talks about risk taking and the capacity for adventure — to learn from experience and not to be overwhelmed by change. Gandhi emphasised that a man never loses until he ceases to struggle. While being talented is an important component of success as it is more likely to make you persevere, talent comes to fruition with support from teachers, mentors, or coaches. Leaders gravitate to others who share their cause and they are good communicators, bringing others on board. They risk pain, rejection, and loneliness and have the capacity to stand up to scrutiny

In more recent times we have come to realise that there are qualities of leadership and personal success that are additional to academic competence and also to Gardner's qualities of framing, reflecting and using leverage. These qualities include the elements of emotional and social competence. Like many others such as Gardner and Sternberg, Salovey and Mayer and Goleman have tried to explain why it is that some people who have scholastic ability do not succeed in life while others with less scholastic ability do. They have come up with the concept of emotional intelligence. Salovey and Mayer defined intelligence as "the ability to monitor one's own and others' feelings and emotions to discriminate among them and to use this information to guide one's own thinking and actions" (Salovey, Bedell, Detweiler & Mayer, 1999, p. 189). This form of intelligence was deemed to be a better predictor of success in life than the traditional scholastic forms of ability. The emotional intelligence quotient (EQ), in contrast to the intelligence quotient (IQ), consists of non-cognitive capacities and competencies that are used to cope with environmental demands. The components are intrapersonal and interpersonal skills, adaptability, and the ability to manage stress and general mood.

The EQ ability model defines intelligence as a set of abilities that involve the capacity to perceive and reason abstractly with information that emerges from feelings. Daniel Goleman (1998) includes concepts such as self-awareness and impulse control, persistence, zeal, self-motivation, empathy, and social expressiveness. He claims that IQ accounts for only 20 per cent of factors that determine success in life. Likewise, he asserts that academic intelligence has little to do with emotional life. A whole host of factors, including what he describes as emotional intelligence, account for the greater part of an individual's successful transition through life. He points out that there are different ways of being smart, and emotional intelligence is one of them. The price of what he calls *emotional illiteracy* is too high and can be seen in the levels of depression and despair experienced by people. The good news is that emotional intelligence is not fixed at birth, it can be nurtured and strengthened.

Emotional competence is made up of two major components, personal competence and social competence. The former includes the ability to be self-aware, to regulate the self and to be motivated. Motivation consists of achievement, commitment, initiative, and optimism — pursuing goals despite setbacks. Personal competence also encompasses emotional awareness, or the recognition of how our emotions are affecting our performance, as well as accurate self-assessment, a sense of our strengths and limits, and self-confidence that provides the courage to move forward. People with this type of competence are described as knowing "which emotions they are feeling and why, realise the links between their feelings and what they think, do and say; realise how their feelings affect their performance and have a guiding awareness of their values and goals" (p. 54).

Leadership Styles

According to Goleman, most effective leaders have a high EQ. Additional qualities such as a positive temperament, passion for pursuits and having the support of others also contribute to leadership capabilities.

Two different types of leadership have been identified — *transformational leadership* and *transactional leadership*. Transformational leadership occurs when the leader stimulates interest among colleagues and inspires followers to view the world from a new perspective. They motivate others to look beyond self-interest towards interests that will benefit the group.

In contrast, transactional leadership is when the leader rewards or disciplines followers with regards to performance. Transactional leaders emphasise work standards, assignments, and task-oriented goals. However, it is transformational leaders who receive higher ratings for effectiveness and satisfaction.

Transformational leaders are more behavioural and less emotional when dealing with stress and conflict. They demonstrate an internal locus of control, that is, they take responsibility for their actions, and have self-confidence and self-acceptance as well as clear goals to which they aspire.

Coping

In addition to theories of temperament, personality, and intelligence, there are theories of coping that describe our reactions to the environment (Frydenberg, 2002). We can use productive ways of coping, such as working hard, staying optimistic, or dealing with problems. There are also non-productive ways of coping, such as blaming oneself, ignoring problems, keeping to oneself, or worrying. What coping research tells us is that we can learn to cope. In fact, we can all learn to do what we do better.

How we cope is a way of describing how individuals adapt to their circumstances. It is a way of understanding human endeavour from a positive perspective, where we consider people's capacities rather than their disabilities or lack of abilities. In recent years coping research has been extended to take into account human strivings and goal pursuits. That is, the way people establish goals, plan their steps to achieving those goals, and organise their environment to reach the desired outcomes. This includes the pursuit of worthwhile goals, that is, goals that are valued by the individual or in the culture. Additionally, there is a striving to reach one's potential, or the capacity to do one's best and achieve growth. This is generally known as proactive coping.

Proactive coping is a future-oriented coping strategy. Individuals anticipate potential stressors and act in advance to prevent them. To that extent, proactive coping is positive, in that difficult situations are seen as challenges rather than as threats, harm or loss. In proactive coping there is planning and self-regulated management of goals. Individuals generally build up skills, friendships and supports. Proactive copers build up goodwill and credits with people and monetary or resource savings that can be used to create a path of action and opportunities for growth. Proactive coping can offset stress before it occurs and is associated with behaviours, including planning, goal setting, organisation, as well as the utilisation of social resources.

While the actions in preventative coping and proactive coping may appear in the same behaviour — such as the acquisition of skills and accumulation of resources or planning activities — the difference is that individuals using preventative coping strategies when under stress may assess a situation as being a threat, whereas proactive copers would assess it as being a challenge. Proactive copers have a belief in their own capacities, at least to be resourceful and gain support when required. They are likely to be ambitious and tenacious in their pursuit of goals, and create opportunities rather than be restrained by circumstances. They generally do not turn back from their goals when confronted with setbacks, but use their coping resources to overcome obstacles, find support, or choose a different path leading to the same goal. Additionally, they are able to find meaning in the situation at hand.

The characteristics of a proactive coper are not all that different from those of a leader. They believe that they are able to utilise resources, whether they be external or internal. That is, they have the capability to achieve their goal and call on the assistance of others to assist them.

The proactive leader possesses the inner resources necessary to cope with demands. These resources include the ability to plan coping strategies, seek social support from others, and envisage success. To that extent, proactive leaders are solution-focused. They adopt a balanced view and do not seek to allocate blame. These leaders use proactive behaviours such as goal setting, and are self-motivated to attain particular goals. The proactive leader takes responsibility for their own growth and chooses their path of action according to their values. There is a focus on continuous self-improvement in pursuit of the self-imposed mission. Thus the capacity to have a vision and the qualities of goal-setting, goal-getting, continuous striving, and seeing obstacles as a challenge to be overcome, all make for desirable qualities in leaders.

Thinking About Leadership

Having touched upon some issues to consider when thinking about leadership, it is time to delve into the stories of some present-day Australian leaders. These leaders come from a variety of backgrounds and work in differing fields. As you read each profile consider the questions in the boxes below and over the page to help you reflect on what these leaders' stories can tell us about leadership and coping. Think about what can be learned from the stories and how they might relate to your own life and future. Think about what inspires you in the leadership profiles you read and try to reflect on your own coping practices and the way you deal with leadership.

Leadership Questions

- What is leadership?
- Can it be taught?
- How do you differentiate leadership from character?
- Is leadership a choice?
- Which leadership styles are most effective today?
- How do leaders lead?
- What do leaders do?
- What qualities do leaders possess?
- Whom do they lead?
- Why do you admire them?
- What aspects of a leaders life do you feel develop their leadership potential?
- What forms of support would you like to see in your school to help young people develop leadership skills?
- In what area of your life do you see yourself as a leader?
- In what area of your life would you like to become a leader?
- What is your vision as a leader?
- What forms of support do you need to make this possible?

Coping Questions

- What challenges were faced by the leader?
- Have you faced similar challenges?
- How would you face such challenges in the future?
- What strategies would you use to cope with such challenges?

Productive Coping

- How would you establish goals?
- What supports would you turn to to achieve your goals?
- Who would you turn to?
- How would you approach that person?
- What additional supports do you have?
- Would there be a group or an individual who can help you to achieve your goals?

Setbacks

- What is a setback that you have experienced?
- How did you deal with it?
- How would you deal with it now?

References

Csikszentmihalyi, M. (1997). *Finding flow.* New York: Basic Books.

Csikszentmihalyi, M., Rathunde, K. & Whalen, S. (1997). *Talented teenagers: The roots of success and failure.* Cambridge: Cambridge University Press.

Gardner, H. (1997). *Extraordinary minds: Portraits of exceptional individuals and an examination of our extraordinariness.* New York: Basic Books.

Goleman, D. (1998). *Working with emotional intelligence.* London: Bloomsbury.

Frydenberg, E. (2002). (Ed). *Beyond coping: Meeting visions goals and challenges.* Oxford: Oxford University Press.

Plomin, R., Scheier, M.F., Bergeman, C.S., Pederson, N.L., Nesselroade, J.R., & McClern, G.E. (1992). Optimism, pessimism, and mental health: A twin/adoption analysis. *Personality and Individual Differences, 13,* 921–930.

Salovey, P., Bedell, B. T., Detweiler, J.B., & Mayer, J.D. (1999). Coping intelligently: Emotional intelligence and the coping process: In *The Psychology of What Works.*, 141–164. Oxford University.

Sternberg, R. (1985). *Beyond IQ: A triarchic theory of human intelligence.* New York: Cambridge University Press.

Ann Sherry AO

by
Lucinda Holdforth

> Ann Sherry was the first female CEO of a bank in New Zealand. Currently the CEO, Westpac New Zealand, and Group Executive, Westpac New Zealand and the Pacific, Ann is a former CEO of the Bank of Melbourne and First Assistant Secretary of the Office of the Status of Women in Canberra. Ann is a member of the Board of The New Zealand Institute and a member of the New Zealand Business Council for Sustainable Development. She was awarded a Centenary Medal in 2003 and an Order of Australia in 2004.

Ann Sherry's story will not appeal to people who like stereotypes. A career including prison welfare, the trade union movement and anti-discrimination policy is hardly a normal prelude to a stellar rise in the banking sector. A passion for social justice is not normally regarded as compatible with a drive for shareholder value.

Yet today Ann Sherry is routinely nominated as one of Australia's most influential business people. Ironically, her success now sees her reside in Auckland as CEO of the Westpac bank, New Zealand. Before this she was CEO of the Bank of Melbourne and Group Executive, People and Performance, in the Westpac Group. Sherry has shown not only that it is possible to reconcile the apparent opposites of a warm heart and a business head, she has been at the forefront in demonstrating that compassion and inclusion can actively contribute to a stronger corporate bottom line.

But it's not only Sherry's career path that confounds all conventional expectations. Her personal story is equally surprising.

Sherry was born in 1954, the eldest of three daughters in the Queensland country town of Gympie (about two hours drive north of Brisbane), where her parents owned the local pharmacy. "I think there was something about growing up in the country that was quite liberating," she recalls. "You grew up without a sense of fear or constraint. I learnt to ride — we'd bring our horse from the paddock and ride up the main street of the town into the yard of our house."

Sherry spent her early school years at Gympie Central Primary. When asked if she had an early sense of ambition, Ann shakes her head as if in puzzlement at the very idea. Nor did she have a particularly strong sense of social justice. On the contrary, she was naughty, sociable, and outgoing. She read voraciously, but she was not scholarly. And her favourite things were holidays. "Once a year we would load up the car and do the Chevy Chase thing — we would do the car holiday. By the time I was in my early teens we'd travelled all over Australia — Cairns, skiing at Kosciosko, Melbourne. It gave me a fantastic sense of difference, of variability and space ... and place."

When the time came for Sherry to attend high school the family moved from Gympie to Brisbane. Her parents bought a big pharmacy in the middle of town and Sherry went to Somerville House, a well-regarded private school for girls. Sherry remained outgoing, happy, bright, and lazy. And she might have stayed that way.

But then, things changed.

> I was in year eight or nine at high school when they announced over the school system that we should stay away from the city because there's been a gas explosion on the corner of Queen and George Streets. That happened to be where my parents' pharmacy was. So of course I went roaring into town. And literally a whole section of the city had been damaged by an underground gas explosion.

Sherry's parents were unhurt, but several people had been injured. And the pharmacy itself, in which her parents had invested so much, had literally been destroyed. This ushered in a difficult period. Both parents became wage-earners to support the family. Sherry's father took a job as chief pharmacist at one of the public hospitals.

And that proved to be the least of the challenges at this time.

Sherry recounts the dramatic event quite simply. "When I was in Year 11, my mother got Ross River virus and ended up paralysed — a paraplegic." Although she eventually recovered the use of her legs, Sherry's mother was in hospital for a long time and in a wheelchair for longer. At the age of 15, the free and easy eldest daughter became, of all things, the responsible woman of the house. She ran the home, organised the meals and looked after her two younger sisters. When asked how they responded to their elder sister's new authority, Ann is emphatic that whatever her younger sisters thought of her was quite beside the point: "I didn't care. I was mother."

For a year, Sherry tested many of the limits — she skipped school lessons; she drove a car, although she was well under legal age. "I used to drive everyone around ... , if we needed to do some shopping we'd all get in the car and off we'd go. I'd drive. I loved it." Ann Sherry, respectable banker, laughs now at the memory of her younger, lawless self. "Dad didn't know ... one of the rules of illegally driving is you do NOT crash the car..."

When Sherry finished high school her primary goal was financial independence. "As soon as I finished school I wanted to get out ... which is why I did radiography." Quite simply, after those years of domestic upheaval and responsibility: "I was out of there!" But radiography was always an unlikely choice for the sociable Sherry. Her summation of the job says it all: "Meet nice people and watch too many of them die." Sherry says now, "It just wasn't for me".

It wasn't just the nature of the job that she objected to. This was the first time Sherry encountered a big, inefficient bureaucracy. It made a lasting impression on her.

> The structure of the hospital drove me mental. The inequity of it! Inexperienced doctors would give us instructions that we thought were wrong. But we had no choice, because answering back was not part of the way hierarchies worked in hospitals. I railed against it. Virtually all the radiographers were women and all the doctors were men. So you could just see the ridiculousness of it, the lack of respect. I was angry.

After two years Sherry left radiography and went to study at the University of Queensland. She started off majoring in computer science and pure maths. Of computer science she recalls: "I spent the whole semester sticking holes in cards with a straightened paper clip thinking, *If this is the New Age, it's going to have to happen without me.*" But the economics class she took as an extra subject proved an eye-opener. "There was debate and intellectual stimulation. Suddenly I thought *Oh my god!* I discovered there was a whole other world out there which was fantastic."

Ann also discovered fellow student Michael Hogan. They married when she was just 20 years old. She still laughs with delight at the irony — for years she had declared that marriage was a complete constraint and she would never subject herself to it — yet she married younger than most of her peers. As Ann recounts the story of her life and career from this time on, it is remarkable how often she prefaces her anecdotes with "we".

During those early days the young couple lived on the $30 a week student allowance. Sometimes they ran out of money and Hogan drove cabs. In the ultra-conservative environment of Queensland under Premier Joh Bjelke-Petersen, Sherry and Hogan also became politically engaged. Sherry became very conscious that there was no anti-discrimination legislation — and that women were still treated as second-class citizens. In those days a woman seeking an abortion actually had to fly interstate. Hogan volunteered at the student radio station (4ZZZ) at Queensland University, which was one of the main voices of youthful opposition.

When Ann was 21 years old she gave birth to a much-wanted baby son, Nick. Michael and Ann were young and fit. The pregnancy had been completely healthy. All the grandparents were excited about their first grandchild. But Nick was born with Down syndrome.

At this point Sherry's voice becomes carefully neutral:

> It was so unexpected. There was no indication during the pregnancy, just nothing. Suddenly at the hospital the doctor appears going, 'Ah, sorry to tell you that your baby's got Down syndrome.' The first advice we were then given was to get rid of him. They basically said to us in a patronising way: 'What can be done is we'll just take him away and he'll go into an institution and you'll have another baby.'

Her reaction to this offer was characteristic: "I've just had a baby, you dickhead." She resumes her matter-of-fact demeanour. "But that was what happened back then, they thought they could take him away."

For the young couple the event was "character forming in the extreme," Sherry says.

> We just had to band together. Sometimes we felt like we were in a bunker together almost fighting everybody. That period really sorted out the sheep from the goats. Some people disappeared from our lives, other people came into our lives. Both our sets of parents really struggled with it. My sisters were fantastic. And we had a band of largely gay male friends who turned up at the hospital with cream cakes and tea.

Sherry and Hogan made a conscious decision that Nick would be as capable as he could be. Sherry did two hours physio with her son each day. She made sure he walked and stood up straight and had good posture. None of it was easy. Nick was sick a lot in the first couple of years. He'd have a sniffle one minute and pneumonia the next — and they'd all be at the hospital an hour later. But when he came out of that early, more critical phase, the family adapted itself. "We got into the groove with it and said *Right, we're on this path now...*"

Nick's arrival ignited Sherry's passion for social fairness. Whenever Nick confronted discrimination his mother went into battle. Sherry says, with pride: "I forced the local kindergarten to take him, despite the fact that I had a delegation of parents on the second day suggesting that he didn't belong there." She still marvels at the face-to-face prejudice Nick encountered. Even when he was a baby, people would openly stare at him and point.

Sherry acknowledges she was profoundly affected by the prejudice against her son. She says she became "like a turtle, a shellback". Today there's still a steely quality under her warm demeanour: you sense the warrior lurking under the business suit.

After Nick's birth the doctors ran a series of tests, but they could find no reason for the Down syndrome. They encouraged Sherry and Hogan to have another baby — they said it would be "good" for Sherry. But, in the absence of an explanation for Nick's condition, Sherry and Hogan weren't prepared to take that risk. And, in any case, Sherry recalls what she told the doctors. "I don't have babies for therapy," she said bluntly.

When Sherry was appointed CEO of Westpac New Zealand in 2003 and announced to Nick that "we" were all going to live in New Zealand, he replied, "No, *you're* going to New Zealand". For the first time, Nick wanted to live independently. Both Sherry and Hogan consider their first few months in New Zealand the hardest time they've endured as a family since Nick was a little baby. Sherry laughs, "We had separation anxiety! I mean, how could he possibly get by without us!" She recalls, "I said to him, 'Why won't you come?' and he said, 'It's time I breathed my own air'."

Mission accomplished.

When Sherry finished her degree in 1977 she applied for, and was accepted into, the Graduate Program in the Commonwealth Government. Because of Nick's needs, she took a position that allowed her to remain in Brisbane. A job outside of Canberra is rarely a stepping stone to bureaucratic success, but this proved to be a valuable experience. The curiously named Department of Productivity, with Ian McPhee as Federal Minister, was focusing on future-oriented research. Ideas that wouldn't gain wider currency for some years were being investigated. Sherry conducted studies into participative workplace practices and the impact of technology on organisations. She examined ways people were thinking about jobs in different parts of the world. Already other economies were seeking ways to bring more women into the workforce. She was beginning to bring together in her own mind the threads linking social fairness and inclusion with high-performing organisations and societies.

In 1981 Sherry was offered a post-graduate scholarship at Warwick University in the UK. The family packed up and headed off to an English winter, but were totally unprepared for the bleak and bitter landscape of Coventry. Sherry swiftly reconsidered. With typical decisiveness, she abandoned her scholarship. She and Hogan took Nick back to London.

"I worked for a group called the Apex Trust. They got jobs for ex-offenders — so I started working in the English prison system." For Sherry, this experience proved as powerful an education as any stint within the academic cloisters might have been. Sherry worked in the Borstals, the notoriously harsh institutions for young offenders. She saw the primary 'crime' of most of her clients was that they were male, poor, and black, usually West Indian. The atmosphere was particularly tense because the Trust was located on the edge of Brixton, where massive race riots had recently taken place.

Sherry worked on two Apex Trust projects. The first was a program to find employers who would take on the young offenders when they came out of prison. The second involved going into the prisons and training the young men and boys to be 'job ready'. "This," says Sherry, "was a huge eye opener." The boys were so deprived they didn't even know how to use a phone, let alone how to pick one up and call a potential employer.

Hogan, meanwhile, went to work in the North London Polytechnic, running the student union. The president of the union was Iraqi, the secretary was an exiled black South African. Hogan and Sherry became part of a world of refugees and political exiles. They became exposed to ideas and issues far removed from their Australian experience.

And then, bringing these experiences with them, they came home.

Back in Australia from late 1982 onwards, the momentum of Sherry's career rapidly picked up, though it was never an unbroken ascension to the top. Sherry's curriculum vitae shows that she moved between various roles. With typical pragmatism she explains why:

> I've hit plenty of barriers — but you either get around them or you go in a different direction. So I only hit my head against a brick wall once, I don't need to go back again and again and again. If things aren't working and people throw up barriers and I can't get around them — then I do something else.

Indeed, Sherry might well have gone down the path of a political career were it not for one particular set of barriers firmly put in her way.

> After I worked in the trade union movement for a few years and the elected positions started to come up again, my male colleagues decided I was probably too high risk to put up for election. So I decided, well OK , I'll go and work in the Victorian Government.

Sherry worked for the Victorian Government for a number of years. In 1992 she was promoted to Director, Children and Family Services, with responsibility for more than 780 staff and a budget of over $70 million. And in 1993, many years after her first invitation to join the Commonwealth Public Service, Sherry finally came to Canberra, not as a lowly graduate, but as Head of the Office for the Status of Women in the Department of Prime Minister and Cabinet. Her achievements there included developing a national policy on women's superannuation, leading to action to protect small superannuation holdings.

And then, in a life of change, another big transition.

In 1994 Ann Sherry left public service to join corporate Australia. As Head of Human Resources Management in Westpac Bank she became responsible for the recruitment and management of a large banking workforce. It was as if all the experiences and learning she accumulated over the years had suddenly found a fertile field for action.

Sherry introduced a range of measures to attract and retain staff. She oversaw the creation of sexual harassment guidelines and procedures. She established a disability employment program. Staff communications became more open and consultative. Family friendly policies were pursued. Sherry is well aware of the irony — after many years in the public sector unsuccessfully advocating paid maternity leave, she was finally able to achieve this important goal at Westpac Bank. When the Bank introduced paid maternity leave in 1995 it attracted a massive wave of positive publicity. Other companies swiftly followed Westpac's lead. New standards in employee relations were being created.

Sherry's success in making the transition from the State and Federal bureaucracies to corporate life is both rare and remarkable. In 2001 the Australian Financial Review's *Boss Magazine* named Sherry as one of Australia's "True Leaders". One of the panel, Les Fallick, director of Gresham Private Equity, said, "If you look at the change in the employment policies inside Westpac, and the way it's managing its staff, I think you'd see huge change, which can be directly associated with the arrival of Ann Sherry."

Today Sherry is CEO of Westpac New Zealand. She's changing things there, too. When she first arrived she made it her business to visit branches around the country. Staff were amazed — no-one from head office had ever taken the time to talk to them before.

Sherry is also at the forefront of the movement known as Corporate Social Responsibility. She not only encourages staff to engage with their communities, she herself is personally active. One endeavour she closely follows is Indigenous Enterprise Partnerships in Cape York, which aims to facilitate the creation of a real local economy and therefore help local Indigenous people free themselves from the depressing cycle of welfare and low self-esteem. This engagement has also included entering a mentoring relationship with Tammy Williams, a gifted young Aboriginal leader who, like Sherry, grew up in the Gympie region of Queensland.

Looking back, it's not hard to see why Westpac wanted to recruit Ann Sherry — with her unique background and track record she was ideally placed to bring reforms to the way Westpac managed and motivated its people and, by extension, its customers. What's perhaps more interesting is why Sherry took the risk of stepping outside the public sector to join a big corporate. Sherry has strong views on this. As she explains, when women fought and struggled for the vote in the 20th century, they were demanding the right to influence the key organising principle for national life — government. Government was by far the single most important factor shaping outcomes for individuals and communities. But in the 21st century we live in a globalised world, a world in which governments have receded from many parts of national life. And, just as responsibility has been delegated, power has also been dispersed. The biggest beneficiaries have been big corporations. Big corporations were always important. Today they matter more than ever.

> Think about it. Whatever we do, we rely to a very large extent upon the quality of our corporations. Perhaps we work directly for one. Perhaps we own or work for a small business, in which case we probably contract with, or consult to, large public companies. We might choose to work in the not-for-profit sector — in the arts, or philanthropy — but, nevertheless, increasingly we must turn to big corporations to provide us with funding and expertise in support of our aims. As contributors to superannuation, we are effectively required by the law to invest in large corporations for our retirement incomes. And, of course, whole communities rely upon the investment decisions of large companies to decide their futures.

With such power, and many more freedoms, corporations are no longer just the passive instruments of government directives, but also potentially active agents of economic and social change. In Sherry's opinion, what corporations do, matters.

> It's a worthy cause to run a profitable organisation on behalf of staff, shareholders and customers. It's a great responsibility to deploy the large scale resources, to mobilise the large numbers of people, to make a tangible difference. It's a great privilege to run a first-rate company with threads extending right throughout the community.

And Sherry is particularly keen for women to feel that it is not only personally appealing, but also morally valuable to aspire to leadership roles in big corporations.

> I believe that getting women into business leadership roles will be both a sign of positive change to the status of women — and a stimulus to that change. Through the resources of big corporations, women in leadership roles will have the opportunity to make a major contribution to the economic and social wellbeing of women, men, families, and commu-

nities in ways that would be impossible to achieve as isolated individuals. Yes, you can choose to vacate the field. You can try to lead from the middle. Best of all is leading from the top.

A discussion about leadership styles with Ann Sherry is mercifully short on jargon and long on common sense. When asked to describe her own approach, she pauses. "What kind of leader am I? Energetic. Passionate. And, yes, pragmatic. I trade off all the time. If you can't get there the way you want, try another way."

It's not surprising that Sherry is often asked for advice and regularly sought out as a mentor. She says she is very happy to talk to people, but generally reluctant to take on the considerable time burden of a formal mentoring relationship. Tammy Williams was an exception. Sherry says with admiration, "Because she wouldn't take no for an answer!"

And it's fair to say that Sherry's no-nonsense style is not for the faint-hearted. She has a low tolerance for corporate self-pity or political game-playing. Sherry says, "People will go on about why this or that person will be favoured above them. And I say, *What are you doing to make it obvious that you should be selected for that job next time the position comes up?*" Some aspirants no doubt retreat from the prospect of being mentored by Sherry with a sigh of relief.

Sherry demurs at the notion of formal mentors in her own past, but she warmly remembers those people she has worked with over the years who have taught and influenced her. "When I first went into government in Victoria, George Brouwer was the Head of Premier and Cabinet. For some reason he spent a lot of time with me, teaching me how to write briefing papers and all the things I didn't know how to do." She adds appreciatively, "He gave me time and that made a huge difference".

Another influence was Dr John Paterson, the outspoken and reformist Secretary of the Department of Health and Community Services in Victoria. "He was a strong individual and a courageous bureaucrat. If he thought something was right he pursued it, even though he sometimes came unstuck," recalls Sherry. She also mentions "Carmen" [Lawrence] and "Joan" [Kirner] — two women who rose rapidly to senior positions in public life — and who suffered dramatic public reversals. She adds, with meaning, "I also watched what happened to them. That was a big lesson".

But today, Sherry finds some of her most profound leadership inspiration outside the work environment.

> I work hard, but I don't work hard all the time. When I've got things to do I'll work until I've got them done, and then I'll have some time off. I've always had holidays and they

often inspire me. We sponsor some kids in Uganda whose parents have died of AIDs. We went to see the people who find the kids who need help. You just think – I've got more influence than these people, and yet they are doing a really direct thing of benefit. After the tsunami, I just wanted to get on a plane. I listened to interviews with young medical students who went and directly helped. That's inspiration.

Asking Sherry about her future elicits a surprising response. She doesn't talk about corporate ambitions or board memberships or financial gain. She talks about change.

I look around and think, there's so much still to change – in Nick's world, the work world, my world, the outside world. So much. [Her voice intensifies as she speaks.] A goal for the future for me would be to use the influence I've got to make a difference. Whether it's to give the people who work for me a much better sense of possibility for themselves, to engage in the work I'm doing for Indigenous communities, to the extent of being able to say that there is a different set of possibilities because of that engagement. My relationship with Tammy is about that. Imagine if I can give her a sense of possibility – 20 years before I got it. She can change so much in her own community. But also, she could become influential on an international stage. She could have completely different opportunities open up for her as a result. My ambition is to take what I've got and to make it work the best I can for me on one level, but also for the people I engage with – and there's a lot of them."

The Queensland town of Gympie is perhaps best known for its Big Pineapple. But it was once a goldmining town. As a little girl, Ann Sherry used to play at digging for gold around the mine shafts and mullock heaps. A fitting start for a future banker perhaps. But this unusual business leader had the foresight to appreciate that the real nuggets of gold lay in empowering the people around her – to succeed for themselves, to contribute to their workplaces, to make richer companies, and to generate happier communities.

Perhaps the best way to sum up Sherry's achievement so far is to quote from her favourite definition of leadership. It comes from Professor Rosabeth Moss Kanter of Harvard Business School. Moss Kanter says: "Leaders leave the world a better and different place; they lead people in new directions to solve problems and make new things happen. They stretch people to achieve things they didn't think were possible. They challenge assumptions, chart new directions and inspire others with the power of their vision. They make heroes out of all the people who have worked with them."

Ann Sherry has already made Australia a different and better place. And you get the distinct impression that she is only just beginning.

Peter Garrett AM

by
Kylie Miller

Peter Garrett is the Federal Australian Labor Party member for the seat of Kingsford Smith in NSW, and shadow Parliamentary Secretary for Reconciliation and the Arts in the Australian Parliament. He sits on the House of Representatives Standing Committee on Aboriginal and Torres Strait Islander Affairs, and the Standing Committee on Communications, I.T. and the Arts. Previously he was vocalist, co-lyricist and dynamic frontman for Midnight Oil for 26 years. Peter served two terms as President of the Australian Conservation Foundation. He received the Australian Humanitarian Foundation Award in the Environment category in 2000 and in 2003 an Order of Australia for his contribution to environment and the music industry. He is a director of the Chifley Research Centre.

"It's better to die on your feet than live on your knees."

Peter Garrett — rock star, lawyer, surfer, activist, politician, Christian, husband, father — conscience of a generation. For nearly 30 years, Garrett has danced on Australia's stage, first as the lead singer of rock band Midnight Oil, then as a Senate candidate for the Nuclear Disarmament Party in the 1984 Federal election, president of the Australian Conservation Foundation (ACF), and as a tireless crusader for environmental, anti-nuclear and Aboriginal causes.

As a public figure he has been the angry voice of a generation. Voted one of the 20 most admired men in the world by the readers of an American magazine, and ninth on a list of the top-10 most influential Australian humanitarians, in 1998 the National Trust declared him one of Australia's Living Treasures. At the height of his fame, *Time* magazine dubbed him a "walking icon of outrage". As acknowledged by an interviewer during a promotional tour in 2000, Garrett "falls into the category of having done pretty amazing things for three decades, so we don't bother with the CV". It would be a rare Australian who hadn't heard of Peter Garrett.

When asked to describe Garrett, one of the singer's closest friends, former Triple J deejay, campaign manager for the Nuclear Disarmament Party (NDP) Senate bid and now Midnight Oil's website designer, Mark Dodshon, is, not surprisingly, glowing: "He's brave, he's loyal, he's strong, he's intelligent. In a nutshell that's it ... He's a complex person, and yet on another level he's a very simple and straightforward person."

It is one of the many contradictions found in the public Garrett. He is simple, yet complex; carefree, yet cares deeply; democratic, yet mildly dictatorial; passionate, yet peaceful; quiet, yet oh-so-loud; spiritual and intellectual, yet practical and grounded; serious, yet fun-loving; organised, yet disorganised; childlike, yet deeply responsible. And perhaps most apparent, he has a huge public profile, yet a private life he treasures and carefully guards. The private Garrett is inaccessible to all but a handful of his closest friends.

In person, Garrett is an imposing figure; some two metres tall, his shaved, angular, skull-like head, loose, rubbery, pink skin and mobile features contributing to an ageless appearance. Seemingly a body composed of all limbs, he lopes in the slightly uncoordinated gait of the very tall. He is down-to-earth, patient, and generous with his limited time.

Everything he does, he does with gusto. Over lunch with friends, he apologetically admits that he doesn't eat eggs, the result of a childhood plagued by food allergies, then promptly tucks into the proffered gourmet omelette with the relish of one who needs fuel to sustain a relentless energy. Forget the allergies — food, he agrees, is one of life's great pleasures.

In an interview, Garrett speaks softly, leaning forward to make a point. He takes time to answer a question, thinking deeply. When the answers come, they are measured, almost poetic, every word seems to count. In conversation he's more relaxed, gesticulating with his arms and hands to make a point, asking as many questions as he answers and listening intently to the response, nodding when he agrees with a point.

Garrett has an ability to make those around him feel special. He seems genuinely interested in what you have to say. A people person, with charisma to burn. It's an intensity that inspires huge loyalty. A sometime Oils crew member tells of how he first worked with the band as a roadie at the tender age of 16. Now, 13 years later and well into a career as a film colourist, Justin Heitman has been known to take leave from his day job to work for the band when they visit

Melbourne. So trusting were they of Garrett's sense of responsibility that Heitman's parents signed the guardianship of their teenage son over to Midnight Oil for the duration of the 1987 "Diesel and Dust" East-Coast Australian tour, to enable him to accompany them on work experience.

"Midnight Oil saved me. They really did," Heitman says of his relationship with the band. Garrett inspired him to change direction and talked him out of quitting school. "I would have dropped out for sure if it wasn't for Peter. But he was such an inspiration to listen to, he's just so educated, and I thought, wow, that is fantastic, and here I am wanting to drop out of school! If he says it's a good thing, it's got to be right. I still look up to him as someone who I'd like to be proud of me like a father would be of a child."

Australian Democrats Senator Natasha Stott Despoja, the youngest person ever elected to the Australian Parliament, and one of the few politicians Garrett nominates among those he finds impressive, says Garrett's foray into federal politics in the mid 1980s had a big impact on her, particularly when she saw the major parties unite to block his path. "Peter Garrett is an enduring role model for many Australians — especially young Australians — and has been a constant source of inspiration for me. His creativity, his passion, and his unshakable commitment to environmental and social causes has helped encourage many of us to fight for a better, greener and fairer world," she said.

It is hard to separate Garrett, the man, from Midnight Oil, the band he has fronted since the 1970s. The band runs its business as an absolute democracy; all decisions unanimously agreed. The Oils' manager, Gary Morris, who has been with the band for 24 years and is among the handful of people who know him best, says Garrett is a thoroughbred, one in 100,000, who demands and receives from those around him the dedication, ingenuity and principle he demands of himself.

"His principle is what you have to deal with. Dealing with the man is really not a problem, but dealing with the principle, that is the criteria for his cooperation ... His principle is the firewall, and few there be that make it through," Morris says.

"Pete is on a stage in everything that he does in his public life, but he writes his own script and he directs it all, and he takes it all up with his convictions. But by the same token it is not contrived, it has to be there because he has a genuine sense of duty to make sense of his life to himself."

His convictions make Garrett a formidable foe in debate, Morris says. "He's a very deliberate and specific, extremely logical person. Every word that he speaks he makes himself accountable now and in the future."

Midnight Oil's financial controller, Craig Allen, says the band's few permanent staff are treated so well that they want to give back 120 per cent. Allen can't imagine the day when he no longer wants his job. "They are just so great to work for," he says. "If there was one word I had to use to describe Pete it would be integrity."

The Oils inspire similar devotion from their fans — and it is appreciated. When a diehard American fan flew from the US after seeing pictures of the "Real Thing" tour on the band's website, one of the members put him permanently on his guest list so he wouldn't have to pay for entry as he followed the tour. According to Allen, the move was typical of the band's generosity.

So how did Garrett become the man he is? As he told a group of final-year school students at a leadership forum in Melbourne, his mother, Betty, and his grandfather, Len Collin, both played roles in the type of person he became, not so much in what they did, but the way they went about it.

> My grandfather just worked in his garage, in his workshop, and listened to the radio and listened to the cricket and listened to the Parliament, but he didn't mind me hanging around. And I'd tell him what I was going to do and he'd say, 'Son, if that's what you want to do, if you think that's a good idea, if you think you can do it'. He never said what he thought, but I knew that he thought that at least if I thought it was worth doing then it was OK by him. I don't think my grandfather would have ever been someone who would have jumped into the kind of life that I've had, but while I'm doing what I'm doing, occasionally I just sort of think about him and think about the way he went about his life, the way he lived out his life.

Garrett says he's often thought about what makes people the people they are.

> My own sense is that it's slightly in balance of nature than it is in nurture ... I think I was born this way, but I think that I've worked pretty hard in the second stage of my life to try and bring some discipline and focus to those aspirations. I don't think my life is particularly special, I don't think that my background is particularly unusual. ... I'm not someone who analyses myself a lot. I see myself and I see the Oils as being journeymen, you know, just doing our thing. I'm a musician and I'm an activist and this is what I do.

Although Garrett studied law at the urging of his father, attending the Australian National University (ANU) before completing his degree at the University of New South Wales, he quickly found law was not for him.

I didn't really do science all that well, I was bored by history, I wasn't particularly good at sport, and I regret to say that where I went to school, the choir was very, very low on the status list and very, very high on the nerds' list.

He told a Future Leaders forum in Melbourne: "Law was all that was left, the kind of thing that would make relatives nod and fathers rub their hands in anticipation of a healthy retirement."

He finished an arts/law degree — although not with spectacular success — and now says his life's only regret is not having given more to his studies and less to his surfing during those early years at ANU. But he doesn't regret the degree and, despite practising law only briefly, says his legal background has been helpful to the Oils.

Midnight Oil holds a rare place in Australian history, mostly for its endurance and influence on the world music scene, but also for its ability to bridge the age divide. Fans who started listening to the Oils in the 1970s now take their children to gigs. Everyone seems to have an Oils anecdote or memory.

According to the band's biography, Midnight Oil was born in 1976, the year guitarist Martin Rotsey joined Jim Moginie, Rob Hirst and Garrett, although the band had existed in various forms since 1971. Bass player Bones Hillman joined in 1987, the third bassist to play with the band. Gray Morris, who has managed the Oils since their inception after meeting them as a young surfer in Sydney's northern beaches suburb of Narrabeen (Garrett was 23 and had long blond hair at the time), makes up the sixth member of the team.

As a group, the band has been together so long that colleagues comment they seem to have developed their own language — a level of understanding that requires little obvious communication. None of the band responds seriously when asked to comment on their frontman. "We'll have to check with Pete," Rotsey jokes. Morris says they are more like brothers than friends.

Garrett laughs when asked if the relationship has turned into a sort of marriage.

I think the foundation of it is a kind of mutual respect for our capacity as a group of musicians to do something where the sum of the whole is greater than the individual parts. The personalities are very different and I think when you've been with a bunch of people in a band for that long they see the best of you and the worst of you ... I think I'm pretty demanding.

With the Oils, the mission was a simple one.

To write a kind of music that was very grounded in the Australian experience where we all lived, which wasn't afraid to walk out on a plank, holding up an idea or even a political judgment to an industry which is, despite its flashiness, inherently conservative and reactionary, and to take control over our careers and see if we could survive. Now we've survived.

Thanks to the profile he built up in the band and credibility built on years of hard work, Garrett has loomed large on Australia's political landscape, his interest in green politics piqued by a deep concern for the future.

Why did I become concerned about the environment? How did I end up as president of the ACF? It's such a basic, banal answer. I got sick of surfing in sewage. Very simple. I went surfing, the water got really dirty, I got sick of hearing guys complain about it, I said we've got to do something about it, let's find other people who are working on it and we did and away we went. And that's the campaign that started the clean-up. It's not finished, but the water of Sydney is substantially cleaner.

Garrett has since gone on to spearhead, or work behind the scenes, on some of Australia's biggest environmental campaigns, including the protracted battle against the Jabiluka uranium mine in Kakadu National Park, and the fights to protect Queensland's Shoalwater Bay and Jervis Bay in NSW. During this second stint as ACF president, which began in 1998, Garrett took on the battle against genetic engineering and genetically modified food.

One of the foundation's biggest achievements under his leadership has been in building partnerships with community and business groups previously out of reach to the environment movement. In 2000, the ACF announced a union with the National Farmers Federation in a campaign to tackle salinity, an environmental issue of huge concern to both parties. Later in 2000, when the Australian Governor-General Sir, William Deane, launched the ACF's "Blueprint for a Sustainable Future", business leaders and heads of industry were invited — and attended. It was a rare moment of solidarity, uniting leading Australians with diverse, and sometimes conflicting interests.

So what does Garrett think about the state of Australia in the new millennium, politically, socially, environmentally?

That's a really big question. [Can he sum it up? — Long pause.] Yes. [Long pause.] There's a good deal of wealth in some quarters, some extraordinary creativity and vitality. But carrying across that I sense a lack of common under-taking about what we want the country to be, and a sense of unease and anxiety partly among youth, also among people not sharing the riches. [Does it worry him?] Yes, it does. It worries me hugely ... The range of public opinion and discussion of the really serious issues in Australia is quite low, and when I say serious issues I don't mean intellectual issues. I mean the things that ultimately are going to determine the kind of lives that everybody lives, that our successors live.

While Garratt's rock star status, distinctive appearance and political stands have given him huge recognition as a leading Australian, along with the many honors, he says he doesn't court the attention and remains sanguine about the hype.

The trick is don't believe the hype. Especially about yourself. [laughs] It's a by-product I think of living this way. Because of this very public stance people develop high expectations that I could probably never meet, but at least they know what I stand for. And everyone's at liberty to agree, disagree, join, walk away. I don't mind.

Being placed on a pedestal, or "are they anchors around your ankles?", brings with it elements he loathes — criticism, the ugly face of a monster keen to lop the top off the tallest of our tall poppies. He sees it as an unfortunate and, arguably, inevitable part of the life he has chosen.

There's a really strong human nature thing to try and amplify somebody or something, and then people react to that in one of two ways. Either they want to pull it down or they want to get iconic about it. Now I don't have much problem with that, it's just that I'm not like that myself, that's not how I see myself, so I just see myself as going about my business, and I find it a bit strange that people make more of it than they need to, either way. So of course if you get hugely flattered you feel OK about it, but then if you get hugely insulted you think, oh, what did I do to deserve that?

Garrett speaks publicly on Midnight Oil and the environment, but rarely about himself. To interview Garrett is "like sitting an exam", wrote one profiler in 1990. "Like extracting teeth" was how another described the experience. Over the course of several meetings, this particular interviewer finds him to be friendly and helpful, if occasionally guarded. He speaks slowly, each point well considered and accompanied by an explanation about how it was reached. Dodshon says Garrett has put no limitations on what his friends may reveal, but he is surprised Garrett agreed to participate in the first place. "He's not someone who seeks attention," he explains.

Morris says there are two Peter Garretts — the public Garrett (or "the office of Peter Garrett" as he puts it), and the private Garrett. But he says not to expect to "crack the kernel" of the private Garrett, explaining that the few allowed within the circle will respect his walls. Besides, he says, it's boring. Not worth writing about. Garrett in private, he says, is just an ordinary man, doing ordinary, everyday things.

Garrett himself is frustrated by the way people assume they know him. Despite his public profile, he is deeply private, fiercely protecting his family and personal life from the scrutiny that accompanies such celebrity. Little has been written about Garrett the family man. The man, who with his German-born wife Doris, decided to move his three daughters from Sydney's northern beaches in the mid-1990s, partly to give them privacy and a better life on a property in the semi-rural NSW Southern Highlands. It is here Garrett likes to hang out with family and friends and live his private life.

> I'm pretty hard working. I'm not too fussed about being a dag and just hanging around at home, having a cuppa tea and sitting under a tree and kicking a footy around and playing a bit of cricket in the backyard. I prefer being outside than inside and being able to do something physical, whether it's walking in the bush or surfing or working or whatever.

Garrett grew up in a close and loving family, a closeness reflected in his own family life. His three daughters adore him, and his marriage to Doris, which he has described as hugely important to him, is undoubtedly a key influence. References to her pepper his conversation. During days off on tour, Garrett, once a wild man of rock, flies home to spend time with his family. He chuckles then gives a deep hearty laugh as he reflects on how times have changed and the band has mellowed with age. No longer can he come off stage, high on the rush of performance, and call friends in the middle of the night. "They are all getting old and have families and jobs," he laments. They would be sleeping. Not up for a late-night muse on the ways of the world. It means earlier nights and less of the post-gig revelry that was once a part of his rock star life.

Garrett enjoys company, but doesn't socialise a lot. He has a large circle of loyal friends, many of whom have known him for years. His range is wide, from rock stars — including the members of Irish supergroup U2 — to former and serving politicians and internationally famed figures in the conservation movement. Garrett suggests David Suzuki when asked about those who might comment on his influence. The list includes the executive director of the ACF, Don Henry, his ACF vice-president, Penelope Figgis, former Australia Prime Minister Paul Keating, and editors of Australia's music street press. Others come forward to talk about a man who has inspired them.

Paula Jones, a long-time fan of Midnight Oil who now handles publicity for the band and for Garrett individually, is typical of those happy to venture a view. Jones met Garrett in 1984 when she worked as a volunteer with the Nuclear Disarmament Party. "Peter does his utmost to accommodate the myriad requests that pass over his desk," Jones says. "He has taught me to be more patient and to assess and contemplate rather than rush into rash decisions. He also encourages those around him to take time out to smell the roses."

Garrett's influence, in a wider sense, has been profound, exposing a generation of rock music lovers to environmental politics, but he says getting a message out is not what drives him. Rather, he lives his life according to a personal set of beliefs. If people choose to follow, respect, admire, agree or disagree, that is their prerogative. He simply strives to avoid hypocrisy and live the life he preaches.

> I'm not actually trying to convince people of the rightness of wrongness of a view at all. I'm just saying what I think and trying to live it out. It's not something that's in my way of thinking about how I live. If you started to think about it, to begin with you'd be making a huge set of assumptions about a whole lot of people you don't know. Each person is very separate, very shaped by a whole set of experiences, with intelligence and the ability to work things out themselves. I really don't like judging books by their covers. I'm not so interested in analysing myself, but I have thought a lot about how to try and move things forward, how to get the best out of myself and the best out of people ... Sometimes you get bits of it right, sometimes you get bits of it wrong, but I think it's all about intentions.

In Garrett's case, tragedy has also played a formative role. Clues to his personal tragedies come in the lyrics of "In The Valley", an emotional ballad first recorded on the *Earth and Sun and Moon* album and repeated on the 2000 release, *The Real Thing*:

> My grandfather went down with the Montevideo, the rising sun sent him floating to his rest ... My father went down with the curse of big cities, traffic tolls and deadlines took him to his peace ... When my mother went down it was stiff arm from Hades, life surprises and tears you like a southerly" — *"In The Valley"* (Jim Moginie/Peter Garrett/Rob Hirst).

Garrett rarely talks about the death of his parents, but most of those who speak about him raise it as an issue. Garrett's father, Peter senior, died of asthma — "the curse of big cities, traffic tolls and deadlines" — during Peter's first year at university. Within a few years his mother was also gone, trapped in an upstairs bedroom when the family home burnt down. Garrett, who had moved home to finish his law degree in Sydney, was unable to save her.

Mark Dodshon, one of Garrett's closest friends since the pair met while studying political science at ANU in 1971, has no doubt the tragedy had a big impact on his friend's life and outlook. Over a few years, Garrett's priorities were forced to change from a fun-loving, party-hard teenager who, with Dodshon, crawled through the scaffolding surrounding their under-construction residential college to choose the best side-by-side rooms, and who relished his morning breakfast at the nearby Catholic women's college under the watchful eye of the "imposing Sister Tarantula", to a serious and responsible young man struggling to help support two orphaned younger brothers. "By the time the fire brigade had come Pete was out on the front lawn, and he actually thought that both his brothers had died in the fire as well. But then each of them arrived home having unexpectedly spent a night out," Dodshon recalls. Garrett had to break the devastating news.

The tragedy also sparked a long period of financial hardship, with the three boys washing taxis and cleaning squash courts at night to make ends meet. Money was very short — Garrett was at university and his youngest brother was still at school. It was a difficult and traumatic time for them all.

Garrett had always worked hard, but his resolve to complete his studies was reinforced. And the economic hardship forced a big change in his life. He was forced to take responsibility, with two orphaned younger brothers to consider. For all his success and generosity, Garrett has never forgotten the value of money and what it is like to be without it.

Morris believes the tragedy and the shock it caused engendered in Garrett a rare appreciation of time and life: "A day is a very valuable thing to Pete and he doesn't want to waste it. Whether or not that has come out as a result of that horrible experience ... He makes every day very important," he says. "I often imagine Pete, when his kids were much smaller, fighting with Doris for the soap and face cloth to take care of them because he needed that in his day. Pete views time in the same way as most people view the stock market. It's an incredible asset that should never be misused."

By the time his parents died, music was already a big part of Garrett's life and Dodshon feels the pain started to come out in his live performance: "Pete tends to downplay it, but he used to scream a lot on stage ... I used to think where the hell does that come from?" Dodshon recalls. "I can't think of the right word, cathartic's probably the best. It just seemed to come from somewhere so deep inside it, it was like an exorcism. He was just letting go in a huge way. And when Pete used to scream in the early days of Midnight Oil the whole crowd would just be frozen to the spot! They were pivotal moments in an Oils performance — it was such an extraordinary thing."

Extraordinary is also a word chosen by Penelope Figgis, the softly spoken vice-president of the ACF, to describe Garrett's energetic performance style — a style that sometimes caused momentary panic: "When I nominated Peter (for the ACF presidency) I had never met him and I wasn't a follower of rock music, so I had never seen him perform ... and so I nominated him and we were very thrilled that it all got up," Figgis explains. "Very soon after that I saw a film clip of him performing and I immediately turned to my husband and said, 'Oh my God, what have I done!' Here was this person leaping around like a mad thing."

Figgis still has never attended a Midnight Oils concert, but quickly realised Garrett's value both as a person and to the conservation movement: "I really like him enormously. At a purely personal level we are good friends," she says. "He is a very unusual person because he has lived in a world that, for many people, is associated with appearances, with materialism, you know, wealthy rock stars, extravagances, and often irresponsibility. Trash yourself with drugs and trash yourself with excesses in various forms, whereas Peter has lived in that world and thrived in that world and been a star in that world and yet is completely different. He is a deeply serious person. He's someone who really thinks about the long-term future of the society in which he lives."

Figgis believes religion plays a part: "We never talked about that a great deal because he knows that I'm not a Christian ... but he's a complex person and religion is part of that that complexity."

Garrett himself believes he has always been a spiritual person, and close friends admit to long conversations and philosophical debates with him on the subject. But, as with all matters, he respects the beliefs of others. For Garrett, religion is very personal. He would never try to convert people to his views and doesn't discuss it publicly.

Figgis laughs when asked if she would agree that Garrett displays conflicts: "It is true that he's an absolute democrat, but he has a deep impatience with people who he perceives to breach good process," she says, diplomatically. Sometimes his impatience and "mild dictatorial manner" have been known to rub the "robust" democrats of the grassroots green movement up the wrong way. But his intelligence, knowledge and hard work on often "unsexy" issues engendered deep loyalty among ACF staff.

Despite a friendship spanning 30 years, Mark Dodshon still marvels at Garrett's energy and influence, talking of the many unpublicised meetings Garrett attends at the highest levels of government: "In half an hour Pete can do a lot, face to face with anyone ... Only Pete really knows who he's spoken to about what and when and what happened, but he does do some extraordinary things ... You just think, well thank heavens there is someone like Pete around."

Phillip Toyne, who convinced Garrett to take on his first ACF presidency when he was the foundation's executive director in the late 1980s, says he's always valued Garrett's constancy: "He's not a populist who just grabs an issue because it will promote either he or his band. He's put in years and years and years of hard, dedicated work on things, and that's the real test I think of integrity."

Garrett and Toyne first met in the 1980s. Several years later and with a new job as executive director of the ACF, Toyne struck on Garrett as an ideal new leader for the foundation, when its serving president, Hal Wootten QC, quit to head up the Royal Commission into Aboriginal Deaths in Custody. "I thought the future of the environment movement had to be with young people, and to talk to young people we had to find somebody that they would relate to, " Toyne says. "He was the sort of person who commanded a great deal of respect from politicians and Prime Ministers and others. He continues to be very effective at communicating with people, and the media, of course, were attracted to him very substantially."

Between them, they managed to raise the profile of the foundation to new levels, attracting new membership and drawing attention to issues in a way that the green movement could previously only dream of. Toyne thinks Garrett's return to the foundation in the late 1990s, courtesy of ACF executive director Don Henry, was an inspired move at a time when it is harder to entice people to give their time or cash to an environmental cause. Toyne believes Australians are still worried about the environment, citing concerns about genetically modified food, air and water quality, but it's harder to entice them to do something about it.

Garrett, in an illustration of his political smartness, has recognised the trend and spends his time talking with business leaders, lobby groups such as the farmers and companies, including many never previously aligned with conservation causes. "What they are basically saying is well if government isn't responding what we'll do is work around government and use business and the economy," Toyne says.

The cross-fertilisation of his two most public roles has no doubt helped the environment movement. During an appearance on the top-rating commercial TV program, *The Panel*, ostensibly organised to promote a forthcoming Oils tour, Garrett donned his activist hat, announcing the inaugural "ACF Ironbar Awards", a tongue-in-cheek prize for the person or organisation who had done more through their words or actions to increase the membership of environment organisations. Contenders included a public relations company hired by the Japanese Government to put a positive spin on whaling, the Prime Minister, John Howard, for opposing genetic-engineering labelling, the resources giant responsible for Jabiluka uranium mine, and Wilson Tuckey, the Australian Minister for Conservation and

Forests and Liberal Party member for the Western Australian seat of O'Connor, who "spends most of his time hoeing into environmentalists". Tuckey was the inaugural winner. The message was beamed into the lounge rooms of a massive television audience.

Garrett still loves his music, but says he doesn't listen to much any more — "I just don't have the time" — but his radio swings between Triple J and Radio National mostly, and occasionally to the classics or his local radio stations. He recently collaborated with iconic Australian cartoonist Michael Leunig on a Melbourne symphony production of *Peter and the Wolf.* But Midnight Oil remains his real love.

According to Toby Cresswell, the editorial director of "Terraplanet," publisher of the streetwise music magazine, *Juice,* Midnight Oil are one of the most influential bands ever to spring from Australia, playing a role in the development of such international high-flyers as REM and U2. "Internationally I think Midnight Oil are probably one of the most well recognised, one of the bands that people would most associate with Australia," he says. "They have got a strong musical vision. I think they are universally respected, for their ethic, relationship with the audience, the way that they have practiced what they have preached."

Of his ill-fated 1984 bid for a Senate seat with the Nuclear Disarmament Party, Garrett says he expected the defeat as soon as he learnt that Labor had done a deal to prevent preferences flowing his way.

> Once the Labor Party decided to do the rat and exchange their preference with the Libs we knew that the chances of getting up were extremely low, even though my vote was very, very high. They did me a favour as we all know.

Dodshon, who worked as Garrett's campaign manager for the Senate bid, says the defeat caused only a momentary disappointment before the pair realised they had achieved the best possible outcome — catapulting the issue on to the national stage without forcing Garrett to move to Canberra, something he would have hated. "He has all the politicians' skills, apart from hypocrisy, and he's an extremely personable person," Dodshon says of his friend, "but going to Canberra then would have been a truly horrible experience for him and he knew that."

Garrett and the Oils had always been interested in social justice issues, but the "Black Fella White Fella" tour of remote and outback Australia with the Warumpi Band in 1986 proved a watershed moment, exposing the group to experiences that had a profound impact, resulting the in politically charged and most commercially successful album *Diesel and Dust.* The lead singer of Aboriginal rock band Yothu Yindi and a former Australian of the Year, Mandawuy Yunupingu, says hearing *Diesel and Dust* inspired him to learn music.

"That's the album that made me want to write songs," he says. "When I started writing songs, the Oils were my band's mentor." In 1988, Yothu Yindi toured the United States with Midnight Oil. Yunupingu remains an admirer of Garrett: "He's helped Aboriginal music, he's helped Yothu Yindi, he's helped the Warumpi Band, and his connection with the movement in Aboriginal issues has been quite profound. I wish there were a lot more people like Peter Garrett around."

At the Sydney 2000 Olympics closing ceremony, before an international TV audience of billions, the Oils donned clothes emblazoned with the word "sorry" as a protest at Prime Minister John Howard's refusal to formerly apologise for previous government and church actions that resulted in a 'stolen generation' of Aboriginal and Torres Strait Islander children being separated from their families under the then government welfare policy. Yothu Yindi followed it up with a performance of their politically charged hit, "Treaty".

Perhaps it is another contradiction, but while an ACF colleague may praise Garrett's past promptness and efficiency in chairing sometimes unruly environment movement meetings, the Oils' sometime tour manager, Craig Allen, jokes that, "the only thing you can be certain about Peter is that he'll be late".

Perhaps it is simply an inability to do all the things squeezed into his schedule, but sometimes his tardiness appears to stem from a child-like appreciation of nature. Instead of arriving on time for a sound check, Garrett might be found outdoors taking in a sunset. He draws pleasure from simple things: desert wildflowers blooming early after unseasonal rain, sunrise, walking in the sun, sleeping outdoors, snug in a swag as the wind howls above. He loves the outback and the red dirt, revelling in the chance an outback tour with the Oils gave him to sleep under the stars in a hired "Rolls-Royce" swag.

Garrett has little sense of direction, explaining it away as the result of a lifetime of travel. He's always in new places, so never knows where he is, he says. Consequently he is usually lost. Material possessions are of little obvious importance and he regularly loses his wallet or forgets his mobile phone. Oils staff have been known to alert hire-car companies in advance to the probability something vital may be left behind when Garrett returns a vehicle.

He has travelled extensively over the years and talks with interest about a range of countries, including Burma, a place he visited years ago and is keen to revisit should the political climate change. One recent overseas vacation was to Cambodia, where a friend works for an international non-government organisation and where, he comments sadly, he failed dismally in an attempt to master Khmer, the local language.

Now over 50 (he was born in 1953), Garrett says he has no great plans for his future. He'd rather take things a day at a time and enjoy the pleasures life throws in this path.

> I'm not someone who's a planner or a schemer, particularly. I'm much more interested in letting the day unfold, in trying to make the best of the 24 hours that's been allocated. Politics is a part of my life, there's no doubt about that ... And even though I'm fairly critical at times about the sorts of decisions politicians make, I do remain a supporter of our political system.

He loves Australia and, having travelled around the world, knows it is where he will always live.

> It's an extraordinary place to be living and I feel very privileged to live here. It has changed a lot in some areas and in some areas it hasn't. It's a more selfish society than it was, which I think is something that we are really going to have to face up to soon. There'll be much greater numbers of people depending on much smaller numbers of people to look after them, with the ageing population, so we are going to have to very radically review our idea of age and welfare and what it really means to live a life. Is it to go out in fury for 20 years and then do nothing for the next 35? It's not how I'm going to live.

The future of the Oils, too, is not something he can plan. "That's a question no-one can answer, least of all me," he says. The band works as a team. All the members have separate interests and musical projects, but when they unite they are a powerful force.

On stage, Garrett is on fire, face contorted and mobile, long arms punching, fingertips splayed, his body twists and turns as those endless legs stomp in a manic, mechanical beat. His pink scalp glistens with sweat in the bright stage lights. In the seething, jumping crowd, the sweaty faithful mimic his distinctive style. They love Midnight Oil, but it's Garrett they are really after.

■

Fiona Stanley AC

by
Felena Alach

Western Australian epidemiologist Professor Fiona Stanley, AC is a leading child health advocate. Named Australian of the Year in 2003, she is Director of the Telethon Institute for Child Health Research, Executive Director of the Australian Research Alliance for Children and Youth, and Professor, School of Paediatrics and Child Health, at the University of Western Australia. She sits on the Prime Minister's Science, Engineering and Innovation Council and the Australian Statistics Advisory Council. She has authored more than 200 research papers in peer-reviewed journals and given numerous national and international presentations on the driving forces behind childhood health and disadvantage.

"My dream as an eight-year-old was to sail out on a boat, go to all these islands, inject the 'natives' with something or other that would save their lives, and sail on into the sunset...(laughs)."

Swashbuckling dreams of "The Lone Inoculator" sailing the islands to save native lives were the outset of Fiona Stanley's journey into a lifetime of medical research — a passionate vocational quest that has contributed greatly to her role as a community leader and inspirational figure in Australian science. Her journey is one of determined curiosity to step away from a script governed by the existent possibilities of how things are and explore instead a vision of how things might be.

Early Days: Dreams of Passionate Science
Born in 1946, the young Fiona grew up in a bushland area near La Perouse, south of Sydney. Hers was a free-range world of

independent-minded childhood exploration in an era she reflects on as "the heyday of Australian childhood". The Stanley family home was "one of those little houses you could make holes in the wall of", a small fibro affair among strange neighbours — an infectious diseases hospital complete with leper colony, Long Bay Jail, a retired horses home, the local rubbish dump, and the Bunnerong Power Station. Along with her older brother, Fiona describes a "variously wonderful family life ... a fantastically wilderness kind of childhood, with a very intensively creative pair of parents".

> We weren't in any way wealthy ... but the richness of our life was extraordinary. My father built a boat, a 27-foot ocean-going yacht that we would go out and sail in, in Sydney Harbour, ... and we had this wilderness bush that my parents had the sense to let us run wild in.

In those early days, her scientist father, Neville Stanley, was a doctoral student researching streptococcal diseases. He was later to become one of the world's earliest virologists, working on developing polio vaccine in the midst of the polio epidemics of the 1950s. Fiona's early exposure to science included observing her father working in the lab on mice or with primates, as well as meeting some of the world's most eminent virologists. To the eight-year-old Fiona though, the scientists seemed like "a load of old farts really ... boring old men". Yet this environment of intellectual stimulation in the Stanley household maintained a sense of contact with the world of ideas and things academic, despite the relative remoteness of being situated in bushland.

> No television ... we had radio, we had the Argonauts on ABC radio where we would write articles and had all these competitions, which was wonderful. I had this quasi-aunt, a friend of my mother's, Marjorie Cotton (later Isherwood), who started all of the children's libraries in New South Wales ... so she came up every weekend and brought the next best children's book. And I was banned from reading Enid Blyton, so of course I read them between brown covers in the bed at night...

Gaining an interest in science was inevitable for Fiona in such a household, especially given that her father "absolutely loved his science, and for more than just virology". Neville would read his children fantastic stories by Jean-Henri Fabre about ant and bee colonies and other things that kept Fiona enthralled.[1] It was within the world of books that Fiona's dreams of 'making a difference' through medicine were inspired — the heroic romance of passionate

---

1 Interview by Norman Swan, 2000, as part of the Australian Academy of Science Interviews with Australian Scientists.

commitment and the devoted vocational pursuit of knowledge through struggle and adversity.

> I had three heroes ... all from inspirational books that I read. The first one is very strange, from a book I got out of the library when I was seven ... a man called George Washington Carver who was a peanut scientist in America: he was black, one of the first black scientists. The cotton industry in the deep South was threatened by boll-weevils and lots of other things at the time, and he encouraged the farmers to grow peanuts. This little book ... we got it out of the library about eight times, and then our dog chewed the front cover, and I was so pleased because then we had to buy the book from the library and I'd have it with me ... It was just inspirational, and what it was, as with the other two books, were people who were absolutely passionate and committed about what they were doing, in spite of all the odds. I mean, he used to sleep in a little cot in his laboratory, because he didn't have anywhere to go ... he was just amazing. The impact of all of the people that inspired me was that they were doing science to make a difference, to improve humanity or improve conditions of social issues. The next one was Marie Curie, and I read the biography of her by her daughter, Eve Curie... I must have read that eight,10, to15 times by the ages of about 15. She was inspirational for lots of reasons; I mean, because she was harangued and criticised, but her commitment was unbelievable, in her commitment to making X-rays help the society. And the last one was Albert Schweitzer. I was given a book, as a prize at school, *Albert Schweitzer: Hero of Africa*, the same kind of thing ... If I looked back to my early childhood and adolescence, they were the three things that stick out as inspirational.

Choosing Medicine: The Long Road

After her family moved to Perth and her father took up a position as the foundation Chair of Microbiology (as a non-medical doctor) in the medical school at the University of Western Australia (UWA), Fiona completed school at St Hilda's Anglican School for girls and wanted to go on to study medicine. In this family of research scientists who had experienced being outsiders to the medical fraternity (her grandfather was a geologist in Papua New Guinea, and her brother became a cancer biologist in New York), there was much reservation about Fiona studying for a medical degree as it was viewed clearly as an undesirable option.

> My parents were against me doing medicine, they didn't want me to do it, it was a long course, it was too long for a girl, so few women did medicine in those years .... They

rather thought I should do science or arts or something like that. So I didn't have a lot of role models that were directly associated with me. Except of course my father, who was a scientist. ... Well yes, after I went into medicine I realised that I'd made a mistake, you see, that really I should have done something else. At the end of first-year medicine I thought I wanted to do marine biology. But I was too scared to tell my parents, because they had said I couldn't do medicine, so I kept on going. And then of course I fell in love with it all, and loved everything and adored it. So it just shows you — if I had then gone and done marine biology they would have said, "There, you see, you should have gone and done marine biology all along".

The process of attending medical school was to be a difficult time both socially and vocationally for Fiona, and proved to be an ongoing struggle. The transition from an all-girls school into the heavily male-dominated environment of medical school (with only six girls out of a total class of 100) presented a huge challenge to her social and communication skills. These frustrations became part of a general uncertainty about relating to others, and the social aspects of practicing medicine. This also accompanied doubts regarding the limits of clinical medicine, which thwarted Fiona's longing for certainty regarding the social application of her medical training. This internal dilemma was consolidated by a period of study in Papua New Guinea, where the spectrum of disease problems faced reinforced Fiona's believe in the need for a different approach to these health issues than merely treating the occurrence of disease.

A seed started to grow in my mind — if only you could prevent disease — if only you could find out why it was caused. ... I'd been up in Papua New Guinea as a medical student for three months of the holidays, and had got very unhappy about where I was going in medicine. ... For my final year I opted to do my general practice weeks with Kevin Cullen in Busselton because he was so enthusiastic. Kevin actually forgot about general practice and for the three weeks he just said to me, "Look, you've got a brain, woman. Use it. Get your degree and start making something of your life". He was the first person to say anything like that to me, and I just worked through that final year of medicine — inspired by Kevin and also by Bill McDonald, our Professor of Paediatrics. His inspiration was different. He kept saying, "Yes, there is a child. But that child lives in a family, and it lives in a community, and it lives in a political structure". So I started to get a much better idea of the social casual pathways to disease outcomes, and how profoundly important they could be.

That has stood me in good stead throughout all of my epidemiological training.[2]

With this formative yet hazy desire to seek something beyond the dimensions of general medical practice, Fiona found it difficult to gain information and support to focus direction for her energies.

So for the whole of my medical training, and very early after that, there wasn't a lot of mentoring, not a lot of good mentoring. It's something I feel quite strongly about in my job now is that you need to have people who are enthusiastic and support you, as well as being a role model. I had role models, but ... not any sense of the hands reaching down in support. When I went and got advice from (usually male) lecturers and professors and whatever, they didn't give me the right advice at all. They didn't tell me about the fact that I could apply for NH&MRC [National Health and Medical Research Council] fellowships, and so on. It always came that I had to find all that stuff out for myself. (I would never let that happen to anyone in here now.) And it begs the question ... why wasn't this told me, that you could do these kinds of things? So, it's all about, OK, I know that I want to do this kind of work... please can you help me, how am I going to get there? Of course there's got to be fellowships, and training scholarships, and have you thought of going to this, and have you thought of going to do that ... so in the end my husband played that role. And was just fantastic.

Fiona's first year out as a resident hospital doctor also led her to work with the New Era Aboriginal Fellowship, which offered the opportunity of touring the State on a fact-finding expedition to nearly every Aboriginal mission, reserve, camp, and fringe-dwelling group in Western Australia. This practical education in social environments and health exposed Fiona to the 19th century hygiene poverty that these peoples were living under, and further consolidated her interest towards preventive health strategies.

Fiona began focusing on children's medicine, helping to run the Aboriginal clinic for the Princess Margaret Hospital for Children. After two years, increasingly frustrated with a sense of failure to translate better health outcomes from her work in the face of this dilemma of Aboriginal health environments, Fiona became "incredibly disenchanted" with clinical medicine.

We would bring these very sick kids into the hospital and perform medical miracles, and then we'd put them back in

---

2 Interview by Norman Swan, 2000, as part of the Australian Academy of Science Interviews with Australian Scientists.

environments which of course were causing these diseases in the first place. And I thought ... "there's got to be a different way of practicing medicine".

In an increasingly despondent state of mind, Fiona turned down a registrar position with the Royal Melbourne Children's Hospital and left Australia to travel for a period.

Having by this time met Geoff Shellam — her future husband, who would soon become an "incredibly important" mentor — Fiona's travels eventually brought her to London. Here Geoff encouraged her towards an opportunity to join the social medicine unit at the London School of Hygiene and Tropical Medicine. It was in this environment where, as luck placed her among the top people in England in many emerging health fields, Fiona discovered epidemiology, public health, biostatistics and social medicine. And this proved to be the quantum leap, where "all the lights turned on, when what Geoff calls my 'little motor' started".[3]

> Suddenly I found that there was this medical science that was interested in cause. And that was it. The little motor got going, and it's been going ever since. So I found my path. Previous to this I guess I didn't feel as if I was in control. Things were happening to me, rather than me saying "Yep, this is what I want to do". Until I found this London experience, and this was when I realised yes, this is the decision I'm going to make now, I want a research career, I want to do this, I want to find out about how diseases are caused, I want to do it in the maternal and child health area, because if you can get it right early in life, you're going to make a major difference, and this could be my niche ... I think I've found my way ... And then I started to learn all the things you would need to do to make that happen, the databases I would have to set up, the kinds of methodologies I would have to learn...

This period in the London School of Hygiene and Tropical Medicine offered crucial access to the Office of Population Censuses and Surveys (OPCS) databases for the whole of Great Britain, with record-linkage and birth-defect registers being set up and added into the database. The power of epidemiology and biostatistics became clear to Fiona as the comprehensive assembly and linking of databanks demonstrated their use value in assessing disease profiles in the population.

After an additional year spent in the United States at the National Institutes of Health, building on an extensive network of contacts

---

3 Interview by Norman Swan, 2000, as part of the Australian Academy of Science Interviews with Australian Scientists.

there, in 1977 Fiona returned to Western Australia, as part of the first wave of epidemiologists "trained in Australia, tackling the new common problems that were affecting our society". Initially, return was greeted by a resounding silence from the paediatrics and obstetrics establishment — "... no offer of senior lectureship, research fellowships or anything. I'd been on an NH&MRC training fellowship, yet no-one mentored me about the possibilities of where my career should go."[4] Instead, Fiona began work in the Health Department, in a bureaucratic role as the Chief Medical Officer in Child Health, where she was able to develop networks and databases all over WA.

> I was very disappointed that I hadn't got a research job, but in my two years there I met every midwife in Western Australia and I was able to revamp the entire midwife's database, I was able to link it with all perinatal and infant deaths, I was able to actually start my research — and research infrastructure, if you like.[5]

Research

It was in 1979 that Fiona decided to move to take up a position as a research officer in the new NH&MRC unit in Population Health that was being set up in Perth. This new role allowed Fiona to pursue her love of research, as she and colleagues worked to properly establish a perinatal research group and the Maternal Child Health Research population database.

> What that did was enable me to set up all the population databases that were required to monitor the health of the population and to do research, AND then to evaluate whether you had made a difference. Because, if you have the data, you can say, well, we are collecting data on all these problems in children: has immunisation made a difference here, has intervention with folate made a difference there? ... Not only does it provide the wherewithal to do your research, it provides you with the capacity to evaluate whether you're making a difference in terms of applying that research, and that's what has been so unique about what we've done. Not so much that we're just good epidemiologists, doing good analysis of very important problems, we've actually taken it right from the knowledge, applied it into the community, and then evaluated its impact ... a constant cycle of feedback and the application of research findings.

---

4 Interview by Norman Swan, 2000, as part of the Australian Academy of Science Interviews with Australian Scientists.

5 Interview by Norman Swan, 2000, as part of the Australian Academy of Science Interviews with Australian Scientists.

Fiona became deputy director of that unit for 10 years from 1980 until 1990, and later director for the last few years. During this time in the mid-'80s, the seed of an idea began to emerge from Fiona's frustration with the research environment in WA at that time. Separate researchers were pursuing work across different disciplines, which in fact contained much overlap, but there was no mechanism to facilitate an exchange of research knowledge and methodology. As an epidemiologist herself, Fiona Stanley held strong awareness of the needs for more collaborative and increasingly multidisciplinary approaches to research in order to effectively explore the causal pathways to child/maternal disease. The limits of working in these conditions and relatively vulnerable position of the research programs (adjunct to the other demands within larger hospital and public health structures) revealed the potential of a proper site from which to coordinate some of the separate yet aligned research programs in maternal and child health. Such a facility would enable the cross-referencing of relevant data as well as opening up consultative processes across the specialised fields. Supported by a number of researchers and health professionals, this approach evolved into a clear vision of a world-class research facility dedicated to child health that encompassed a multi-disciplinary approach to major childhood illness. It would be a facility that would bring together research scientists with a whole spectrum of other specific fields (such as epidemiology, biostatistics, psychosocial sciences, cell biology, genetics, clinical sciences, and others). It was an exciting and daunting proposition, yet from around 1986 it seemed "the time was right". As a whole network of colleagues established their interest in supporting such a venture, Fiona became a pivotal player in developing the idea of the institute as a centre of excellence that would also provide a place to foster the next successive generation of practitioners in this field of research.

> And so the other legacy that I am known for is setting up this institute ... I mean, this institute will not be famous because of what I've done, it will be famous for what other people have done in here. Because the better part of what I've created is an environment for other people ... to do their work and to grow, to become great scientists and to do good things.

The TVW Telethon Institute for Child Health Research (ICHR) was initiated in 1990, with Fiona Stanley positioned as founding director. Under Fiona's leadership, the ICHR has grown into a significant player in the medical research field in Australia. In 2004 it achieved more than $16 million in research income, with national and international peer-reviewed competitive grants making up more than 50 per cent of that total, and the joint supervision of 56 postgraduate students.[6] One key thing that ICHR has achieved and gained renown for is the innovative methodologies that have been developed. Having assembled population databases that are considered among the best in the world, a key strategy towards improving public health outcomes is the use of data to evaluate health profiles and patterns of disease, and then apply interventions and evaluate whether changes are effective. This approach furthers a focus on the science of prevention; providing concrete evidence that supports the fundamental effectiveness of applying resources in early, comparably inexpensive stages of intervention, as opposed to the extensive measures necessary to address later manifestations of disease. The network of research expertise at the ICHR enables a matrix approach to evaluating the causal pathways of child/maternal disease, engaging a thorough multidisciplinary process where a complement of knowledges can aim at ambitious research agendas.

Lessons of Leadership

The shift from the idealistic dreams of "The Lone Inoculator" into the role of spokesperson and director of the ICHR is a significant evolution in Fiona Stanley's pursuit of science that makes a difference in the greater social context. Taking up the mantle of leadership at ICHR eventuated in response to the need for a key figure to represent the institute in order to establish the support and funding necessary to turn the dream into reality.

> Oh, God, there've been so many hard lessons ... I mean, the setting up of the institute, and the selling of the idea in the late '80s, I know I didn't do it very well at all. You know, there were so many things that I found very hard about trying to visualise what it was going to be; and I had a vision for it, but how to actually figure out the steps to get there, that was just so hard. ... And there were so many people who kept on saying "Well, you really can't set up a world-class institute in Western Australia". There was not much enthusiasm for it from certain sectors of the medical community. The point is that there were enough people that were enthusiastic, I guess, and it all happened in gradations, ... but there were times that I was distraught at the thought we'd ever get there. As one gets distraught about the fact that one's research isn't going well, that you're never going to find how brain damage occurs in kids in utero, you know, you get very despondent about some things. But then you just think ... if you're on a path like this, this is just absolutely the way you know you have to go! You either climb over those things, you go around them, you think of many different ways. ... My sense is that once

6 TVW Television Institute for Child Health Research Annual Report, 2004.

you are in something that is absolutely the right thing, the fantastic thing, then things happen, serendipity absolutely starts to happen.

The advantages of an environment such as envisioned for the institute reveals a crucial recognition of the value of teamwork: the enormous quantum difference that can be effected through the combined energy, expertise and commitment of a shared vision or goal. Such collaborative enterprise allows for larger projects to be visualised, where the skills and knowledge of many different players are brought in to complement each other — to challenge, refine and enhance each individual contribution. In working towards a project larger than any individual's immediate view, the organisational coherence required to create a solid team framework requires the kind of communication and responsibility that we associate with the function of 'leadership'. A significant amount of energy and vision is required to initiate and maintain team-building to bring each member's work into maximum effectiveness, and to create a structure solid enough to undertake the long, ongoing, and sometimes difficult process of collaborative research. In the classic paradox of leadership, Fiona's own movement into a leadership role was also a step away from hands-on research, and necessarily into more administrative, communicational requirements.

My sense is that I'm not really a brilliant researcher by the standards of Australian or international science ... I've made a reasonable contribution to science, but on the whole the strengths that I bring are of having a big vision, both for research and how research should be organised. I'm a big picture person, and I can see the initial picture, and get inspired to work towards it. ... I think that being a big-picture person is great, as long as you've got enough people in the slipstream who do all of the really important, solid stuff that's going to make it work. I tend towards seeing the big picture, I mean, every 10 years I've changed in a major way what that big picture should be. But why the ICHR has been successful is because I've managed to get around me other people who are absolutely outstanding, who have implemented it. Because you can't have the big picture, and be out there selling it, and implement all of the nitty-gritty ... You delve down into this institute and there's excellence everywhere, not just in the science, but in the administration, occupational health and safety, how we run our staff, how we interact with the media, everything is excellent. Too many people who are at the top don't surround themselves with the best people, and they should. It's the secret of success.

Discussing the importance of this principle to the vision of the ICHR, Fiona identifies the importance of a "culture of excellence" in the aspirations of the organisation. Fiona defines excellence in this context as an individual focus on self-challenge. Excellence is first and foremost a self-choice to continue striving towards integrity in one's endeavour. Once an individual is secure and confident in this process, a fundamental embrace of challenge also benefits from the contribution and inspiration of others, particularly in an environment that focuses on noncompetitive modes of achievement. In Fiona's view, the dream of a centre of excellence for medical and health research was the strategic proposition to enable researchers to best contribute to public health and wellbeing.

In this kind of creative enterprise where there is little of a 'script' to follow, the importance of passion and positivism in a leader is highlighted by difficult, crucial decisions that must be undertaken and for which the collective vision has no easy answers. Quality judgment and integrity in these decisions is central to the trust that any leader must ultimately expect from the community which they represent.

> I'm a person who works very much on positive emotions rather than negative emotions, so one thing I'm very good at is being positive and exciting people and stimulating people to work with me, bringing people along with me, all that sort of stuff. Sharing this vision, and getting people excited about data. If I've got a talk to give on trends in child health, or what's happening in adolescent suicide, or we have a big indigenous research program ... I can feel a whole audience going 'Yes, yes, this is the way to go'. I'm not very good at negative emotions, people say to me, you know, you can't have this grant, we're not going to give you any money from State government ... sure, it's a frustration, sure it gets me down. I don't know how good I am at handling that ... I think possibly what I then want to try and do is go and excite these guys, take them to some kind of level of understanding, level of appreciation. I want to get them excited as well. So that the people who frustrate me, or who are negative, or who are overly critical or whatever, I either try and get them on side, or I dump them. I just don't let them worry me. There's been a lot of that. I mean, when we first started up the institute, everything used to worry me ... if people didn't think we were a great thing, I'd get terribly worried about it. Now it just doesn't fuss me one jot ... if they don't want to come with us, let's move without them. ...

The ability to take people from the specific to the general and make links between a broader view and the integral elements that combine in order to create that picture is one quality that Fiona identifies as something she brings to her leadership role. In discussing important attributes of leadership, Fiona identifies several other qualities she values and aspires to — that a leader be inspirational, a good communicator, be flexible and in particular generous.

> (Sir) Gus Nossal once said to me that one of the most important characteristics of an institute director was generosity. He's absolutely right. I think that one of the things I am good at as an institute director is being generous. And that means being generous with your time. Taking time out to mentor our young Aboriginal researchers is really important, taking time out to find out what's happening to people in the institute and where they are going — it takes time to be generous, actually, to do that job properly.

Offering critical feedback is an honest and clear manner is also a necessary aspect of good leadership. In this way, such feedback maintains a balance of critical appraisal and positive encouragement that can assist in realising the maximum potential of both projects and individuals. As well as recruiting excellence, identifying when decisions and actions must be undertaken by a leader themselves is a central part of the delicate balance of exercising leadership. Other valuable lessons of leadership Fiona describes have been about recognising its limits: that good leadership steps away from the paternalism of 'solving' or 'saving' other people's problems, and instead guides people towards finding their own solutions. This is sometimes best achieved by encouragement, through reminding individuals of what they are good at, and enquiry into how they intend to tackle the challenge for themselves. In this way, the frustrations of certain challenges that seem impossibly difficult can be channelled into their most useful form, sometimes becoming the impetus towards fresh, creative, or lateral approaches to those problems. This is the kind of creative impulse that can transfer itself into a quantum shift in a given situation, such as the kind of collective will that has ultimately realised the ICHR itself.

Leadership in the Community: A Vocation

As well as her role as a spokesperson for ICHR, Fiona has been regularly called upon to enter the realm of public debate to comment and offer the institute's perspective. This is the role of individuals whose authority to speak is considered to have been earnt through dedication, hard work and achievement, and whose contribution to the community can represent a demonstrated public integrity. As a society examines its priorities and resources, the community seeks the comment of such distinguished individuals within public debate for independent thought and the courage to speak accordingly. The social commitment of someone who has dedicated their life-work towards important contributions to public health is the basis on which Fiona Stanley is called on as a public figure. She has become a major advocate for science and research in the community, espousing the strategic benefits of well-placed scientific interventions. Her consistent lobbying of governments to increase funding and support for research is part of a tireless commitment to both science and the greater social body. This active championing has had a key role in the development of the medical and research sectors both in Western Australia and nationally.

As an advocate, the key concern that Fiona Stanley is currently engaged with in her public contribution is trying to promote the use of scientific and research data towards evidence-based policy in both public health and other social justice issues.

> What's driving me now is frustration at the lack of using data and evidence to drive any agendas in health, development, wellbeing, crime prevention, improving educational outcomes ... It's an incredible frustration. It's driving me enormously. Because what people are doing now is putting huge amounts of money and effort into the end of a causal pathway, and not asking what's turning the tap on ... wait until it all happens, and then try and pick up an absolute disaster. That frustration drives me all the time. And it drives me ... insane, but it also drives me into doing something about it. And so that's the really big issue for me at the moment; trying to convince people across all areas, in research, in policy areas, in practice etc ... that they're getting the wrong end of the stick.

Her advocacy of the potential of research data in decision-making emphasises the need for quality feedback information when evaluating the range of interventions that might be considered in regard to the particular problems that present themselves to both social issues and governance.

> It's really about getting enough information, enough data to show the complexity of the causal pathways, and point out the obvious societal interventions that are going to make a difference. It's really tough. Hopefully you'll trigger enough people into thinking along those lines. It's the response arm that's so difficult to do, and researchers aren't good at that on the whole, they just publish and hope that it's going to make a difference. And the difficulty with that is that there's all these little bits of the jigsaw, and someone's got to have a big picture to see where all of the pieces might relate to each other. You know, the question of what kind of picture are we trying to build here, not just what do we have the technology to do that we couldn't do before ...

> Who's looking at the big picture? So who makes those big decisions in society about the balance? That's something that concerns me.

The importance of these questions is crucial in an era where we are redefining fundamental questions about what we expect from government, and what is the best use of the limited resources we have as a social body to shape our future prospects. This is where social leadership, as the recognition of an individual's quality of judgment and experience, are a function of the responsibility they exercise in the public forum. As a scientist and institute director, Fiona observes a clear responsibility towards public discussion and policy development.

> When we go into the political arena, as you call it, we try and get evidence-based policies. People say I am very successful politically because I have pulled in government money, and money for our research building, and I've lobbied the Federal Government to double the medical research budget and so on. But I am very careful to come from an extremely credible position of data with which to inform and influence. This is again Geoff's mentoring; never step outside that, because you'll lose credibility ... When I retire it will be different: I am going to come out and speak on lots of things. For now, I stick to those issues on which I have some data and I won't go beyond that. I think you can only be a good politician for the kind of research you are doing if you stick to that message. Yes, we have tried to influence lots of things, but with good data to support it. We might make mistakes, because sometimes you have to make public health decisions on data that is imperfect. That's an issue, but I think we do the best job we can.[7]

For her contributions with the ICHR to research and the Australian scientific community, Fiona Stanley has been commended with many significant forms of recognition for her achievements, including the Order of Australia, and commendation from the Aboriginal community as a 'sister' to the Aboriginal people for her contributions to Indigenous health. This reflects her aspirations towards integrating research science and a movement towards social justice. She cites her heroes as Nelson Mandela, as well as Mervyn Susser and Zena Stein,[8] who are Professors of Public Health at Colombia University, New York. Despite a brief encounter with breast cancer, Fiona Stanley has continued with an energetic pursuit of her goal of making a difference with her work.

---

7 Interview by Norman Swan, 2000, as part of the Australian Academy of Science Interviews with Australian Scientists.

8 Nelson Mandela, Mervyn Susser and Zena Stein were anti-apartheid campaigners in

The thing that I'm very keen that we should be doing as an institute, but also as a whole area, as a whole discipline, is that public health research, maternal and child health research, whatever you'd like to call it, should actually have a human rights and social justice agenda. And that's what is driving me mostly now. So there's not only what you research, and how you apply it, which should have this bigger social context. ... That's really important for me and I would love to get more decision-making based upon evidence. Decision-making that's going to improve society. I'm very excited about the fact that that's where I am now. Actually I can see, in the next 10 years, that's where I want to be. Being an advocate.

8 *(Continued.)* South Africa. Fiona considers them as intellectual leaders in the philosophy of epidemiology and its analysis. To her, they epitomise the use of data for human rights, such as seen with the symposium in their honour in June 2004, called "Public Health, Human Rights and the Development of Civil Societies." In Fiona's words: "That's the kind of leadership they've provided for the world, outstanding epidemiological research, plus using it to improve society."

Michael Kirby AC, CMG

by
John Heard

In 2006, Justice Michael Kirby will become the longest-serving judge in Australia. He was appointed to the High Court of Australia in February 1996. Previously he was President of the New South Wales Court of Appeal, Deputy President of the Australian Conciliation and Arbitration Commission, first Chairperson of the Australian Law Reform Commission and a judge of the Federal Court of Australia. He has held numerous national and international positions, including Board member of CSIRO, President of the Court of Appeal of Solomon Islands, UN Special Representative in Cambodia and President of the International Commission of Jurists. In 1991 he was awarded an Order of Australia.

In our 'young and free' Australia, a dry continent to which men were once condemned for, among other things, "the abominable crime of buggery", I met with our first openly homosexual Justice of the High Court. The man who bears the name and letters 'Justice Michael Kirby AC CMG' is a member of both a most highly regarded public institution — judge of the High Court of Australia; and a most frequently vilified category of society — a man who has lived with a same-sex partner for many years. As a judge, Michael Kirby is decorated and commands a certain degree of respect, as a gay man Kirby has faced unfair stereotyping, a lifetime of discrimination and the pain wrought by fear and secrecy. People have made assumptions about him. People have gossiped about him. Some of their assumptions are correct. Michael Kirby is indeed non-radical and over 60. In this he resembles numerous other members of the judiciary the nation over. He is very intelligent, displaying a history of academic excellence and dedicated scholarship, and this is how we like our judges to be. But homosexual as well? Two hundred years ago his type were convicts. But Michael Kirby is homosexual, and he is considered, arguably, the most powerful, openly gay man in Australia. To examine what has brought him to such a position of leadership is to explore Kirby's attitudes towards, and experiences of, leadership in the context of an unwavering sense of spirituality, a conviction that scientific innovation and education can liberate the downtrodden, and finally, a devotion to the protection of human rights.

Assumptions and Surprises: Human Rights are Fundamental

Michael Kirby is a Companion of the Order of Australia. He is also, however, decorated with an honour from a much wetter nation. From the same British Isles that once incarcerated Oscar Wilde, gay playwright and decadent wit. Despite professing the same variety of love as Wilde, Kirby received a Companionship of the Order of St Michael and St George in 1983. Whereas in that earlier fin-de-siecle he would have been imprisoned for his kisses, Kirby in our own millennial era is celebrated. The social changes that have forced the reappraisal of societal attitudes towards homosexuality, and the currents that have stirred those changes, are reflected in the life and leadership qualities possessed by this respected Australian leader.

Michael Kirby's leadership success has flowed from the qualities and attributes he is often praised for, and which have seen him find his place at our judicial pinnacle. He is gifted with an expansive perspective, and rather than restrict himself, as may be expected, to the enormous tasks before the gay-rights lobby, His Honour is well-known as an advocate for all human rights. He has said: "One of the problems of gay people is that they don't see the linkages between discrimination against them, and other forms of discrimination. I want to see the linkages."

Such sentiments have led Kirby to a lifetime of human rights activism. His resume is filled with positions with United Nations (UN) bodies and other agencies that have directly involved him in the fight to restore or safeguard the basic rights of oppressed peoples across the globe. Perhaps this interest is fuelled by his first-hand knowledge of the personal tragedy of having one's own rights denied, or perhaps it is borne out of Kirby's firm Christian faith. It is likely a synthesis of the two.

Just as it may appear incongruous for a High Court Judge to be openly homosexual, Kirby's strong Christianity may surprise some individuals. The widely accepted homosexual stereotype does not include a regular churchgoer. Nor does it include an individual who frequently recalls Jesus' teachings from the Bible in an attempt to apply Christian ethics to real-life situations. As with the previous stereotype, Kirby resists such a shallow categorisation. For as open as he is about his love for his male partner, Johan, His Honour is also open about his trust in the love of Jesus Christ and the value of organised Christian religion.

The Religion of Love:
"It's wrong and it has got to stop!"

> Ultimately we are accountable to God, not to earthly creations — Michael Kirby.

> For there are eunuchs who have been so from birth, and there are eunuchs who have been made eunuchs by men, and there are eunuchs who have made themselves eunuchs for the kingdom of heaven — Matthew 19:12.

Eunuchs of the kind initially spoken of by Matthew are fortunately rare in modern life. There are, however, a variety of perspectives regarding the final two types and the relation of these to the condition of homosexual Christians, a category into which Justice Kirby fits. From the perspective of the Catholic Church, the largest religious organisation on Earth, and explained by the Catechism, there is much evil in the persecution and discrimination perpetrated against homosexuals by some community members. On this matter Kirby and the Churches agree. His Honour has also described homophobic violence and attitudes as 'evil'. Others find less cause to object and loudly espouse their detestation of the so-called 'homosexual lifestyle'.

The Catholic and Anglican Churches now distance themselves from extreme insensitive viewpoints on homosexuality as may be espoused publicly from time to time by unbalanced individuals. The Catholic Catechism recognises that "the number of men and women who have deep-seated homosexual tendencies is not negligible" and admirably advocates acceptance of homosexuals with "respect, compassion and sensitivity". It also acknowledges that homosexuals "do not choose their condition". The Catholic Church, however, also prescribes perpetual chastity for homosexuals and calls for gay Catholics to identity the "difficulties they may encounter from their condition with the sacrifice of the Lord's Cross". Through the "virtues of self-mastery that teach them inner freedom, prayer and sacramental grace" such people can "gradually and resolutely approach Christian perfection". Some would describe this as the 'love the sinner, hate the sin' approach, or in the eloquence of Matthew, as "eunuchs for the kingdom of heaven". These facts, taken with the movement of some fractions of the Anglican Communion to ordain and celebrate openly homosexual clergy, may lead one to believe that if there is not peace between the Christian Churches and their homosexual adherents, at least there isn't open rebellion.

It is Michael Kirby's view that this is not the case. The third part of Matthew's passage speaks of another kind of eunuch. Kirby would argue, along with some gay and lesbian Christian groups that homosexual Christians are cast as Matthew's second kind of eunuch. Kirby and these others assert that gay Christians are stripped of a loving or meaningful outlet for their natural sexual desires by the arbitrary impositions of an insensitive Church hierarchy. The Catechism of the Catholic Church also, for instance, describes "homosexual acts" as "intrinsically disordered", "contrary to the natural law" and directs that "under no circumstances can" acts of homosexual union "be approved". Cardinal Edward Clancy has in the past issued a joint statement with his Anglican counterpart, condemning the Sydney Gay and Lesbian Mardi Gras. Far from being an example of pride, or an important forum for presenting legitimate homosexual issues, the Archbishops' statement called the Mardi Gras "an exercise in gross exhibitionism", and an event that "does not merit ... support".

Whatever your view of the Sydney Mardi Gras, it can be recognised by nearly all that what began as a human rights protest march has indeed morphed into a gaudy, licentious spectacle. But the symbolism of the most senior of Australian Catholic hierarchy making a negative statement about the Mardi Gras resonated in many places.

When I questioned Kirby about this reaction to such issues he cited the example of Martin Luther:

> I was brought up within that tradition (Protestantism) to believe, rather boldly really, that you have a kind of hotline to God, that the other, mortal institutions can get it wrong, that you can receive a Spirit, which is bigger than yourself, without the interference of other human beings.

I informed Kirby that these statements sounded foreign to my Catholic ears, and that the majority of Christians, those of my own tradition, have great respect for and put much emphasis upon, the promulgations of 'other human beings'. In fact, the Catholic Church believes that under specific circumstances the Pope is infallible, that he cannot make a mistake. Kirby responded with:

> It is my belief that we should all listen to the point of view of others. The fact that earthly institutions have a view different from your own should cause you to reflect on your own and question your own. You should not arrogantly believe that you have all the truths. The history of the Churches, not only the Catholic Church but also my own church, the Anglican Church, and all the other churches and beliefs beyond Christianity, is that they get into the hands of human beings who are flawed. Sometimes deeply flawed. You've got to keep a healthy scepticism about these things because, what is orthodoxy one day, may be heresy in the next.

Michael Kirby appeared here to oversimplify the enormous leap of confidence (some may say arrogance) such a perspective requires homosexuals to take. It is an almost Socratic 'personal contract', not between man and the State, but between man and his Creator. It is the product of a very Lutheran notion that one does not receive salvation through mortal intermediaries, but brokers it with God by the personal recognition of the sacrifice of Christ and the guidance of the Holy Spirit. Such a belief was natural to His Honour. Others may find rebellion against the codified teachings of their religion; the institutions on earth that purport to dictate the path of redemption for all humanity, harder to swallow. Surely, the decision to voluntarily participate in acts that have sometimes been listed by your Faith as "sins that cry out to Heaven for punishment" would be much more difficult to proceed with than Michael Kirby allows?

When quizzed about Cardinal George Pell's public comments warning of the moral inconsistency of an active homosexual life and the kind of life a Catholic is called to lead, Kirby expresses dismay at such attitudes:

> I am sure that he is sincere in the views that he expresses. His life's experience has been different to mine. If he had had my life's experience, and reflected on it, he might well not have come up with such hurtful statements. People don't chose their sexuality. It is a wrong thing to stigmatise it, or try to put it down. Sadly, that is a feature of the Christian Churches at the moment. But it will change. It's almost beyond my belief and understanding, in the face of modern scientific knowledge on homosexuality, that intelligent people can still hold these views. But they do, and we must take the time to correct their errors. It is the moral duty of people, and not only gay people, to endeavour to do so. I feel a moral duty to do so. I accept my Christian upbringing. I will not allow anybody to part me from it.

Thus, Michael Kirby feels his motivation for religious and social reform is based upon a moral, and indeed Christian, understanding of human nature.

Despite his professed Christian convictions, Kirby has expressed a concern that some may see him as an exclusivist Christian.

> Certainly I was brought up in that faith. I believe that I remain true to my love of Jesus. But I also love people who search for spirituality in other ways — through the Orthodox Churches, Judaism, Islam, Hinduism, Jainism, Sikhism and Buddhism.

He has also noticed, along with George Pell, that:

> The fastest-growing religion in Australia is 'no religion'. There are plenty of non-religious people (including my partner) who have a deep spiritualism and love of humanity. You do not need to find God to find love of humans and indeed animals. Sometimes the God of the Churches or at least the Churches themselves actually get in the way of that search. I have always thought that the global movement for the defence of human rights and human dignity is based on love and is a form of spiritualism. So I do not exclude Humanists from my world.

Here we have Kirby the inclusive, Kirby the Humanist, Kirby as a spokesman for pluralist Australian society. It is Kirby's cast on the basic human need to seek out and attempt to describe the unknowable, something we often term religion. Every reflection of human spirituality is celebrated and valued. Some may interpret such a view as a naïve cultural relativism. Others clamour that it is the mark of a truly tolerant man. Whichever your preference, Kirby's reminder of the negative role that has sometimes been played by organised religious bodies is nothing new. The Spanish and Roman Inquisitions, the desecration of holy places and wholesale slaughter of Catholics under the reign of Henry VIII in England, and the madness that creeps from religious fundamentalism of all types for much of the past few decades support this. There are few who would argue, however, that the current failings of organised religion share any of the malicious intent that has characterised much of the religious evils of the past. Nor is this the view of Michael Kirby. Rather, he acknowledges that Christianity and other forms of spirituality, and even the Humanist movement, foster good relations between humans. Modern psychology has shown us that those who subscribe to these philosophies are less likely to hurt their fellow humans and more likely to respect life in all its manifestations.

Michael Kirby has a great respect for the particular pedagogical style employed by Jesus. He extols the virtues of learning through parables, by explaining complex moral or other theories through the medium of a simplified tale. Parables often have elements that are highly familiar to the intended audience. It is through such simple parables on leadership that Michael Kirby feels we may be able to teach the young to acquire leadership skills. By representing examples of great courage and good leadership in simplified tales, Kirby feels we will be able to pass on leadership knowledge to those who will mature into the leaders of the future. This admiration for parables is coloured by a deeper belief in the value of education. Justice Kirby's educational beginnings, and his continued involvement in the area, read like a parable for future leaders, instructing them in the benefits of learning and scholarship.

Education: Participant and Leader

Michael Kirby, like most young Australians, began his long history of involvement in education as a participant in the system. He proved to be a very good one. He attended Sydney's Fort Street High School, an institution with a tradition of academic excellence. When comparing Fort Street to Riverview, a Jesuit School at which he once gave a notable address, Kirby said:

> It was a sort of, less well endowed, but academically superior, version of Riverview College. I didn't receive a disadvantaged education; I received a very good education. I remember a judge did come to Fort Street (Justice Charles McLelland). He spoke and he seemed a very grave, serious sort of person. I suppose he was a kind of role model to me of the authority figures of society. I wasn't unaffected by that.

It was not long before Michael Kirby began to excel at Fort Street and rose to one of his earliest leadership positions, joining the ranks of the school's prefects. His matriculation result gained him a position at the University of Sydney, and he eventually graduated from the institution with a Bachelor of Arts, a Master of Laws (first class) and a Bachelor in Economics. After quite some time at study, a persistent legal mind with leadership potential was unleashed upon the world.

Something of a hero to human rights and jurisprudence advocates, Kirby has since received numerous plaudits from teaching institutions around the globe. He is the recipient of a number of honours and honorary degrees that recognise either his dedication to the advancement of human rights, or his contribution to Australian tertiary education. Macquarie University, the National Law School of India, the University of Ulster, The University of Newcastle (NSW), The University of Sydney, and most recently, the University of Buckingham, have conferred honours upon him. As a complement to his academic leadership, Michael Kirby has also been closely involved with the administration and guidance of Australian universities, as a member of the governing bodies of the University of Sydney, the University of Newcastle (NSW) and Macquarie University. He served as Chancellor at this last institution for nine years between 1984 and 1993. From 1996 onwards he has been an honorary Fellow of the Academy of Social Sciences in Australia. It is difficult to imagine a leader with such an educational pedigree as Justice Kirby's ever feeling shamed in an academic setting. This makes it important to recall that while he was attending university, general societal attitudes to homosexuality ranged from begrudging tolerance to episodes of outright violence.

Thus, his academic achievements are all the more commendable considering that while he was studying the undergraduate Michael Kirby's sexual orientation was still classified as criminal. Long before the Tasmanian uproar regarding discrimination based on sexual orientation, the United Nations censure, and the subsequent Commonwealth Government Anti-Discrimination Amendments, the youthful Kirby would have been imprisoned for making love with another man. It may be hard to believe that amid the sexual exploration and experimentation common to most people in their 20s, homosexual men like Michael Kirby were forced to choose between living out their sexual preference and displaying affection for one another, or remaining law-abiding citizens. Kirby assured me that initially he belonged to the second category. His first sexual experience was delayed until his late 20s, a fact that he intimated caused him substantial personal pain, and which he feels was unfair and unjust.

In light of these facts and in spite of them, Michael Kirby cherished his intellectual opportunities, and he encourages a robust intellectual vigour in the youth of today. When asked for advice to young people who may be studying at the moment, he advocated a healthy scepticism. Kirby welcomed a concern, especially among those studying legal or political subjects, that the law may truly guarantee justice and equality for all.

'Leadership' and Other 'Boring Topics'

> If we could extract the essence of leadership and bottle it, it would be a product bigger than Coca-Cola — Michael Kirby.

It has been said that leadership is less about being visionary and more about the ability to communicate a vision directly to others. If we think on notable leaders of the past, both great and terrible, we begin to notice that regardless of their particular vision, if they could convince the public that their path forward was best, they gained the favour of their constituents. Michael Kirby is an Australian leader of an exceptional kind. His 'path forward' is professed to be altruistic, to be structured around spirituality, his faith in science as an enlightening force, and his optimistic vision for the future of Australian society. Not only does he excel in the legal profession and in the pursuit of human rights, but Kirby is also involved in ethical debates about the advancement of human genomic technology and is in hot demand to deliver addresses to rooms full of admiring listeners, or to contribute to reputable publications. What are this views on leadership? How does he perceive leadership in an Australia context? What insights into leadership can he offer to younger Australians? Many of his answers to these questions begin with God and end with the law. They concern the "ordinary people" and the "great". They call all Australians to an unwavering standard of moral fortitude. They speak of honour, courage, and love.

> Ancients described leaders as having a charisma, a special grace or talent, that exuded from them as a favour vouch-safed by God.

When questioned about which leaders in the Western tradition he felt embodied such qualities Kirby eschews the choice of a politician:

> I wouldn't normally think of attributing to a political leader as such, charisma. It's a word much bandied around. There's a great need for political leadership, but I would look for something beyond that, and it's often found not in people who are at the top of the totem pole, but people who are lower down, who are working in areas of work that are very difficult.

Michael Kirby suggests Martin Luther King Jr. and Nelson Mandela as appropriate role models for all people. His choice of these two is not surprising given his interest in human rights and belief in the inherent dignity of all human beings. Kirby also, however, cautions against rashly glorifying role models to the point of ignoring their faults.

> Each of them, like myself, had his flaws. Nelson Mandela, for example, wouldn't talk about AIDS while he was President. He could have affected the struggle against HIV in South Africa. He was once asked to do so and he told the people who came and spoke to him about it that they couldn't expect him to talk about condoms, it was beneath dignity. He has changed since leaving office. But what he could have achieved as President!

Kirby then acknowledges one of his own flaws. He spoke of his failure whilst President of the Australian Law Reform Commission to do "more for another minority taught by the centuries to hide itself — homosexuals and others disadvantaged by law because of their sexuality". He lamented the absence of "greater courage on my own part" that may have allowed him to channel more of his energy, and the resources of the Commission, into eliminating some of the legal inequalities that are a reality for same-sex couples. Kirby hastened to add, however, that "courage in those days risked imprisonment and social ostracism".

Faults aside, Kirby lauds his role models for:

> Their courage, and second, because they were people of forgiveness, which I think is very important and one of the chief lessons I learnt from my religious upbringing. Third, they had a spiritual dimension.

Spirituality is an integral part of the kind of leadership Michael Kirby values. He often speaks of some of the people he met during time he spent in Cambodia. These people, whom Kirby describes as "workers for human rights and the betterment of society", had a profound impact upon him. He asserts one example of spiritual fortitude, moral strength, and admirable leadership, in particular. He speaks of a Sister Joan. The leadership qualities he admired in Sister Joan included a capacity for the gentle incitement of others to perform acts of love, a good sense of humour, and saint-like patience. These three qualities, he has said, also inform Michael Kirby's leadership endeavours. His gentle yet insistent plea to Australians to join the campaign to protect the rights of all members of society certainly appears to encapsulate the quiet encouragement of moral goodness in others that Kirby recognised in Sister Joan.

Kirby becomes uncomfortable when discussing his own leadership qualities:

> I feel a bit awkward about talking about leadership in my own case because I feel it tends to aggrandise myself in a way I feel uncomfortable about. I suppose inevitably the fact that I am a Justice of the High Court makes me a kind of leader to contemporary people, at least to lawyers. The fact that I have done a lot of work for human rights makes me a leader of some kind in that area. The fact that I have expressed my opinions about sexuality makes me a leader in those areas. But I just feel awkward about the notion, because it does seem to be blowing your own trumpet.

An interesting statement from a man who is renowned for his willingness to put himself in the public eye and who has been known to air his opinions on topics as diverse as landmines in Europe and breast feeding in Africa. This aversion to self-flattery is a trait common to many Australians. We tend to quickly desert those of our leaders who appear too self-assured, we turn from personalities who appear to be riding upon a wave of their own popularity, and we quickly dismiss those who are bloated with their own self-importance. Leadership in an Australian context, as demonstrated by Michael Kirby's comments, involves little of the self-praise that may be seen elsewhere. The Australian people become disinterested in celebrities who express too much of a self-interest. This may result from the convict history common to some pioneering white Australians, or it may be borne of a distrust of the megalomaniacal tendencies witnessed in the leaders of the nations from which many of our population have fled.

Or maybe it has something to do with Michael Kirby's sentiments. His has a vision of Australia, and Australian leadership, that he claims is egalitarian and honest. It is a vision that recognises the dignity of all citizens and celebrates their potential as leaders of the new century:

> I think a very important aspect of my persona is that I do not feel myself to be better than the ordinary citizen. I came from ordinary citizens. I went to a school with ordinary citizens. I got scholarships that took me to university where I mixed with a lot of ordinary citizens. And I acted, as a lawyer, for ordinary citizens.

Here is also a man conscious of the fact that his position is irretrievably connected with the hopes and aspirations of the Australian population: "I was appointed to do work for ordinary citizens and I continue to do that."

As Michael Kirby would have it, the greatness of a nation can be measured by the calibre of its people. When questioned further about the specific qualities important to those who aspire to leadership positions, the topic of spirituality returns.

> There are undoubtedly people whom, by their example of courage and a spiritual dimension, are people I look up to. My religious upbringing was not unimportant. I was brought up in a Protestant tradition. That is a tradition which is democratic, essentially, and also willing to stand against authority. It holds that, ultimately, we are accountable to God. I think that did have a big effect on me. So I would add Martin Luther to my list of people I admire. Not that he didn't have flaws. For example, he was flawed by his anti-Semitism. But he stood up against a lot of things that we would now see as wrong, in the Church of his age. He took great risks in doing so. Risks to his own life. By his courage, he helped change the world.

Kirby is a man with eyes that flick easily from past to future attempting to learn from previous mistakes to build a better tomorrow. Surely it is for the developing generations of Australia, for the youth of our nation, to emulate at least the passion in articulating a vision shown by Michael Kirby. In this way they may attempt to construct a fairer, more excellent future than the one some Australians have experienced in the past.

Kirby's vision, not surprisingly, includes a greater focus upon scientific exploration and discovery. The conclusions this research shall produce, Michael Kirby believes, will enlighten the prejudiced and eliminate discrimination, two blights that sometimes trouble Australian society. Simultaneously, Kirby urges acts of personal courage to reinforce the benefits delivered by good science. He calls on homosexual individuals to shoulder leadership initiative and reveal their true nature.

It's a matter of people, like me, of whom there are millions
in the world, speaking out. So far everybody's gone along
with this game of silence. It's absurd and it has to stop. But
it won't stop while people who are homosexual or bisexual
simply hold their tongues and go along with the game. I've
gone beyond that. I think it's necessary for other homosexual people to do so and for their friends to support them.

These are tough words. Surely, the process of revealing one's sexual
orientation to a family, a circle of friends, a church community, or
the wider world, would demand major bravery on the behalf of the
individual. In Kirby's own case, however, newspaper articles around
the time Kirby 'outed' himself noted that his statement caused
modest public interest and very little outcry, if any at all. This is
something that he is aware of and thankful for.

There are risks and dangers in doing so. Of course, I'm in a
privileged position. I can do it without losing my job, or losing
all my friends. There are others who are not so well placed.

Despite this, Michael Kirby would argue, courage on the behalf of the
leaders and every member of the homosexual community is necessary if the situation of intolerance and discrimination he feels they
sometimes face is to be fixed.

Basically, it's a matter of spreading the truth and
confronting the mores, which demand silence and shame.
You can't be ashamed of something that God made, or that
Nature made, and what you are. It's like being ashamed of
your height, or your eye colour, or your skin colour, or your
gender. It's ridiculous.

Science and Human Potential: A Vision of Equality

Leadership in an Australian context, Kirby would advocate, requires
ample quantities of courage, personal strength, moral enlightenment,
religious devotion, and unswerving conviction. When we have such
leaders, Kirby believes his vision of a fairer future will become a
national reality. To further effect the process of achieving such
harmony he believes in the benefits of 'good science'. It is a conviction that also informs his hopes for the homosexual community.

Encouraging and promoting knowledge of the scientific
explanations, including about the nature and origins of
sexuality, is the starting point. It's the starting point of all
rational, ethical constructs. To understand what you did, to
understand true nature. For example, so long as people
believe that homosexuality is a 'lifestyle' and that it's
something that is deliberately and wickedly chosen by
people in order to upset devout members of the Church or

of society, then you will have ignorant points of view expressed about it. But when science sweeps away those cobwebs, things will change.

Certainly, the power of truth and knowledge is immense, and the benefits of scientific insight when coupled with moral rigour can change history. The invention of the motor car and the ethical guidelines that form the road laws combined in this way to gift humanity with a valuable mode of transportation free from many of the horrendous dangers that could possibly result from driving. In the same manner, Michael Kirby hopes, research into human genomics and psychological functioning will improve the situation of homosexuals and other minority groups in society. The wisdom learnt from research, Kirby argues, is beginning to erode the basis upon which people may object to homosexuality.

> Science is definitely on my side. The revelations of the nature, origins, and features of human sexuality are so overwhelming today that those who speak against it are like those who speak against the scientific understanding of the creation of the world, or the evolution of human beings and other species.

Stemming from this enthusiasm for scientific inquiry, Michael Kirby holds a number of notable positions in the various scientific fields, including an ongoing term as Governor of the International Council for Computer Communications and a member of the World Health Organization's Global Commission on AIDS, in which capacity he has contributed to debate about possible vaccines for HIV/AIDS. Kirby's special interest though is in genetic research ethics. He is a member of the Ethics Committee of the Human Genome Organisation, a member of the International Bioethics Committee of UNESCO and was a rapporteur at the International Conference in Bilbao, Spain on the Legal and Human Rights Issues of the Human Genome Project (HUGO).

> Basically, HUGO is the ethical watchdog of the publicly funded, scientific body that brings together scientists from all parts of the world who are mapping the human genome, identifying where, on the genome, are the various genes that lead to our being tall or fair or left-handed or prone to Alzheimer's disease, and so forth. The UNESCO Committee is a body established within one of the UN agencies that is trying to formulate the general principles that will guide the global response to the issues of the genome.

Ironically, both gay commentators and religious institutions have cautioned scientists regarding the development of genetic technology, for similar reasons. Both fear that genetic manipulation or 'tampering' with the genome will lead to a new form of eugenics. Both envisage a future where prospective parents will be able to design their offspring, eliminating any 'undesirable' traits or qualities in the effort to create a 'perfect' child. Such an outcome, they argue, would lead to the creation of a genetic lower class, a section of the society born into disease, deformity and suffering because their parents couldn't purchase a brighter life for them. Homosexual commentators fear parents will deselect the theorised 'gay gene' and produce uniform generations of heterosexual humans. This would be an insidious form of sexual genocide they argue. Michael Kirby, however, feels that these concerns can be kept relevant and implemented via involvement with the bodies in which he holds membership:

> I think that, overwhelmingly, the Human Genome Project and the outcomes of it will be to the benefit of humankind. It's no big benefit to have a genetic disease and to suffer premature death or pain from it. The beginning of the steps that will take humanity to curing, responding effectively to genetic diseases (of which there are 5000 major conditions that cause suffering), will be the knowledge of what the genome is, where the genetic conditions are, and how we can go about helping people. But it's true; there are a lot of problems. The possibility that insurance companies can charge extra premiums for people with established genetic conditions, or refuse them insurance altogether, or provide cheaper premiums for people who'll take a scan on a number of genetic tests, or elimination of foetuses (people) with particular conditions. These are major problems and they're only a few of them.

By his example, Michael Kirby shows that only the constructive partic-ipation of leaders in the debate surrounding important scientific developments can yield fairer outcomes for humanity. Leadership in a scientific context therefore involves channelling an avid interest in a particular development into an understanding of the issues surround-ing that technology. By moderately contributing to a discussion of the concerns raised by certain sciences, one can have a positive influence upon the future direction of research, and more importantly, upon the just implementation of the changes brought about by the new developments. Specifically, this approach informs Kirby's involvement in debate surrounding the issues of the patenting and intellectual property protection of human genomic information.

> That is a matter that might come before the court. Whatever my personal stand is, my duty is to give effect to the law. Patenting is statute law. It's therefore a matter where the Parliament will have spoken. My duty will be to try to inter-pret the law, so long as it is within the Constitution. The

Federal Parliament has very large powers over patents of invention. It is basically for the Parliament in Australia to decide. In any case, whatever Australia's view on that matter, it is also going to be relatively insignificant in the global debates about the patenting of life forms. Most of the patenting goes on in the United States of America, where the Supreme Court held that it was possible under the US law to patent life forms. I don't wish to be unduly negative about this. Clearly, the way in which you will get major investments in the pharmaceuticals that will help people with Alzheimer's and other genetic conditions will be by protecting intellectual property.

Similarly, it guides his response to the related issue of the so-called "corporate hijacking" of the new technology and a possible squandering of scientific resources in the production of biotechnology consumer products that will benefit the frivolously rich and not those in most need:

The question of whether the Genome Project will really benefit all humanity, whose genome it is dealing with, or will be concerned with wrinkles, rather than with the issues of malaria prevention, is a major global question. There are many problems. Yet overwhelmingly we should be positive. We should realise that it is not alien to us. The genome has always been there. It is just that in the past 50 years we have begun to discover it.

But, as a leader, one should not be discouraged from an interest in, or enthusiasm for, the benefits to be garnered from scientific developments. Leaders, Michael Kirby has shown by example, are to guide science towards what they feel to be equitable outcomes and positive results. It is the duty of leaders not to take a reactionary stance and condemn new technologies, but to consider how they may be best used to benefit humanity. Leaders must actively participate to safeguard the human rights of individuals in danger of being adversely impacted upon by scientific discoveries.

Conclusion: A Story Still Unfolding

Firmly grounded in his own controversial understanding of the Christian faith, a belief in the ability of humanity to chart our own course towards redemption, a sense of the value and sanctity of human rights, a trust in the benefits of education, an enthusiasm for scientific innovations, and a generous optimism in the future of Australian society, Michael Kirby, the lawyer, the campaigner, the leader, presents something of an example for the youth of our nation. As is so often the case with those who ascend to great places, Justice Kirby has risen above the prejudices and possible discrimination that may have worked against him. He now holds a position where he can best effect what he believes to be positive reform of Australian society. Whether one either appreciates or rejects Michael Kirby's perspective on certain issues, one cannot help but acknowledge his persistence and peculiar success in making his message heard in many and varied places.

In recent years he has continued his involvement in activities upon the international stage, including chairing a Committee of UNESCO that drafted the *Universal Declaration on Bioethics and Human Rights*, adopted in Paris in October 2005. He has also been rapporteur of a United Nations Committee that drafted *International Principles on Judicial Integrity* for UNODC. He serves on a panel of UNAIDS advising on human rights issues of the HIV epidemic. At home he chairs a committee that is bringing together the National Museum of Australia and the National Capital Authority to provide a museum facility in Commonwealth Place, Canberra, on "Defining Moments in Australian History", planned for opening in 2007.

This review of Michael Kirby as a leader has detailed only some of the great variety of roles he has possessed, the most notable omission being details of Kirby's time with the Australian Law Reform Commission. It cannot forecast what Kirby will involve himself with in the future. One gets the feeling, however, that whatever activity Kirby chooses to undertake, the task will be informed by his unfailing enthusiasm. Perhaps one may divine something from Kirby's entry in the *Who's Who*, a publication usually remembered as the one in which he publicly 'came out' as a homosexual. Under another heading Kirby lists an attribute that should better enable one to predict his future endeavours. Listed below "recreations" is a single word: "work".

Author Note

I was a somewhat gauche, closeted freshman when I first met Michael and put together this chapter. Hopefully some of that painful awkwardness has worn off and I am certainly now more honest about myself than I was in 2000. I only mention these facts because Michael Kirby was instrumental in the defeat of both my shyness and my dishonesty. I dedicate this chapter to him: a magnificent correspondent, a good influence and — perhaps most surprisingly — a truly wonderful friend.

Larissa Behrendt

by
Larissa Behrendt

Larissa Behrendt is Professor of Law and Indigenous Studies and Director of Jumbunna Indigenous House of Learning at the University of Technology, Sydney. She is a practicing lawyer and lecturer and has worked with the United Nations. She sits on various tribunals and councils, including the Administrative Decisions Tribunal and the University of Technology, Sydney Council. She is widely published. *Home* is her first novel.

My earliest memory of living in Cooma, a small town nestled in the southern highlands of New South Wales, was walking outside into the frost without shoes on and feeling my feet freeze. I have loved warm climates ever since! But I still feel a great fondness for country towns that remind me of my childhood. My other memory of my early days was arguing with my mother over what I was going to wear. She was a skilled dressmaker and would sew outfits for my brother and myself. She would sometimes change us three times a day, and was always proud that the woman who ran the preschool thought we were the best dressed children in town.

A lifetime of working in social justice has seen that little girl with the cold feet achieve some pretty interesting things. Here are some of the life lessons that matter to me.

Develop good written and oral communication skills.

My mother always read to my brother and I before we went to sleep. She would write out sentences such as "Larissa has a pretty pink dress and she will wear it tomorrow". I would have to copy it on the line underneath, tracing the curves and strokes of her hand. These activities ensured that the values of reading and writing were instilled in me as a very young child. Both my parents have always been avid readers and I grew up in a house that was filled with books. Every night my mother would read my brother and I a story, or we would read to her. Storytelling became a very important part of my growth to adulthood and the very special times that I spent with my mother and brother.

My father was a shift-worker so I did not see him as much as my mother. She was always with us. I thought at the time that she was a stay-at-home mom. I only found out later that she in fact had a part-time job when we started preschool, but because her care was constant and we were never left with strangers, it appeared to us that we had her all to ourselves. I visit Cooma twice a year now for work that I do at the prison, and I always drive up to my old house because my memories of it are so strong and happy.

Do not let others make you feel bad about yourself.

From Cooma we moved to Norfolk Island. My father was an air-traffic controller and he was transferred there for a two-year stint. We lived in a big house that would sigh when the weather changed. Norfolk Island had only one streetlight when I lived there and, if it were overcast at night so the moon and stars were hidden, the house would be so dark that you could put your hand in front of your face and not see it. The darkness made the creaking house seem all the more eerie and my mother was convinced that there was a ghost in it. There are, of course, many ghost stories about on Norfolk Island, most dating back to the times it was a penal colony and life in such an insular society was brutal.

It was at school on Norfolk Island that I first experienced deep racism. Certain children used to taunt me about being black and would call me names that I didn't really understand, but I knew were meant to be derogative. Some of the other children would throw things at me when I walked by. I was confused about this because I did not know that it was bad to be Aboriginal. I asked my mother why people would tease me about it and what was so shameful. She told me that they were just jealous and ignorant and that I had a cultural heritage that I could be proud of. My mother's words of wisdom did not stop me from feeling hurt and humiliated when other children picked on me, but they reassured me that there was nothing wrong with being Aboriginal.

Make sure you spend time with your loved ones.

While the racist taunts hurt, the children involved were small in number and I have many happy memories of Norfolk Island as well. My mother established the first preschool in the area and I can still picture her driving all over the island in her minivan filled with children. My father was the manager of a football team — there were only three in total — that only won one game over the two years we lived there. To celebrate the win he had a party that lasted three days!

When we moved back to Australia it was to Sydney and the first time I had been to a big city. I still remember flying in over all the red tiled roofs, amazed at the sheer number of people.

I finished my years of primary education at a selective school that catered for high achieving and academically talented students. For the first time I experienced flexible learning and a group of peers who were bright, imaginative, and chose to play word games and cards at recess and lunch, or invent original dances to favourite songs. It was the first time I had encouragement to be confident with my abilities — both academic and creative. Leaving this environment to go into mainstream schooling took a lot of adjusting. At the time there were no selective high schools in the area where I lived and my parents thought I was too young to travel on the train to the nearest one.

Not long after I had started high school, my father had a series of heart attacks. He was one of the first people in Australia to have a by-pass operation. It took him months to recover. I remember that my father was sick for a long time and he was on worker's compensation. There was a boy at school who used to always say that my father was a dole bludger and a "lazy Abo". I wasn't happy that my father was sick — he had almost died several times and we had prepared for the worst — but I was pleased that in the long months of his recovery I was able to spend more time with him than ever before. I got to know him better as he talked to me about how stars were made, how different rocks were formed, how things grow, and how the government works.

Understand what life is like for those who are less fortunate than you are.

During that time of recovering his health, my father decided that he would start looking for his family. He knew that his mother was Aboriginal, and that he had been placed in a home when he was five. Over the years, he had lost touch with some of his siblings. He searched through government archives and found a removal certificate issued by the Aborigines Protection Board that showed that my grandmother had been taken away from her family and placed in the town of Parkes. Even more importantly, the certificate showed that my grandmother had a brother, a Sonny Boney. My father then travelled out to Walgett, Brewarrina, Lightning Ridge, Coonamble, Goodooga and Collarendabri to find his uncle. Sadly, when he finally tracked him down my father found out that Sonny Boney had died only three months before my father finally knocked on his door.

My father told me about the policy of removing Aboriginal children and how it had impacted on the lives of Aboriginal people throughout New South Wales and the rest of Australia. He became involved with the establishment of a group called Link-Up, which assisted Aboriginal people find their family, and was able to help others do the same research that he did. It turns out that he was quite lucky to find documents relating to our family in the government archive as there are plenty of instances where the paperwork has been lost. I became very aware through my father's own experience and his work with Link-Up of the many tragedies that had been created by this policy of removing Aboriginal children from their families, especially the psychological trauma that so many of those affected by the policy had suffered. These insights also made me realise how lucky I had been to have a family who loved me and in which I had been safe.

Speak out about things that are wrong, unfair and unjust.

It used to infuriate me that the children I went to school with did not know anything about this past policy of forced removal of children. When I would speak out about these injustices, I think that many of them thought I was quite strange. But I didn't care. I felt strongly about it and my parents had always encouraged me to express my opinions. I became involved with debating and I also did a Toastmasters course. My father also encouraged me to read George Orwell. I read *Animal Farm, 1984, Down and Out in Paris and London* and *Burmese Days*. I didn't understand them all at first, but Dad would explain what they meant. He would also ask me to read out loud whatever text we were studying at school at the time while he cooked dinner, interrupting me constantly to add his thoughts and observations. He would take me to hear other Aboriginal people talk, such as Michael Mansell, Marcia Langton, Gary Foley, Bob Mazza and Roberta Sykes at meetings and rallies.

The 1980s were a very dynamic time in Indigenous politics. It grew on the momentum of the civil rights movements of the 1960s and the radical politics of the tent embassy and the medical and legal services of the 1970s. It culminated in high-profile protests in 1988, Australia's Bicentenary. My house was filled with my father's politics and I learnt a lot from him about my culture, Aboriginal history, and about human rights. I also learnt from him and the many people that I saw speak at community meetings, rallies and universities about the importance of strong, powerful advocacy.

Encourage those around you, especially people who look up to you.

So I grew up with a strong sense of political activism and social justice. I also had a strong pride in my Aboriginality and I knew all about the history of Aboriginal people in New South Wales. I must have seemed unhappy as I tried to fit in at high school. My favourite teacher, Miss O'Sullivan, once said to me, "Larissa, you might not like high school but you are going to love university". Her comment struck a chord with me. I thought it was the most natural thing in the world that I would go from high school on to university, even though

I hadn't really thought about it before and no-one in my family had gone to University.

I began to really admire Roberta Sykes and Marcia Langton around then. Roberta had been to study at Harvard and Marcia had studied to be an anthropologist. Every time I met them they encouraged me and I was thrilled that they thought that my studies were important. They thought I could make a difference if I worked hard. And with my passion for social justice already strong in me, their encouragement translated into a desire to become a lawyer and work to change the system.

Come to terms with the things that have harmed you, survive them, and celebrate the fact that you are strong.

While I was in high school I was sexually assaulted by a member of my extended family. He has since passed away and I have not often spoken about what happened to me, but as I look back on what the hurdles and challenges were for me, I cannot deny that overcoming that was probably one of the hardest things I have had to do. The experience gave me many emotional problems as a teenager and it affected my relationships with men. It gave me a poor self-image of myself and I lacked confidence. I would over-compensate by trying to please everyone and be outgoing. It took me many years to break the bad behavioural patterns that started when I was violated as a young teenager. I tried blocking it out for a long time. I had periods where I was very angry, and I have struggled with an eating disorder and thoughts of suicide as a result. I have since come to learn that these reactions were normal, but at the time I thought that there was something wrong with me and I felt out of control.

But I had the blessing of having loving parents and a supportive brother that I only fully appreciate now I am older. I do not think I would have coped as well if I had not had the benefit of a childhood that was so happy and in which I was encouraged to believe in myself. I cannot say that I have fully come to terms with what happened to me, but I know that I had to accept that it was not my fault, acknowledge that what happened to me was wrong, and to be proud of myself for not becoming more of a victim for it.

Like most women, I have formed relationships in the past with men who were not comfortable having a partner who was strong and outspoken, and I have learnt along the way that you cannot succeed if you are constantly apologising to others for your hard work and deserved success. Speaking out and working hard is stressful and requires strong support. I now appreciate a partner who appreciates me for who I am and makes me feel like I am a better person for being with them.

Start small and build up momentum.

Miss O'Sullivan was right about university — I loved it. I wasn't a star student though. In fact, I failed the first semester of my commerce degree so I switched to another! But I got into a regular pattern of study and worked hard. I became involved with student activities and spent most of my time at the Aboriginal student centre. I met some great people there — Terri Janke and Toni Janke, Lisa Brisco, Anita Heiss, Loretta Kelly — today some of my closest friends and most supportive colleagues. It was during this time that the Royal Commission into Aboriginal Deaths in Custody was taking place and I co-wrote an article with my brother (my first published article) in the university newspaper about police racism. It was called "Bad apples or rotten fruit". It was a small place to start, but I've been writing and publishing my thoughts ever since.

Build up a support network of mentors and peers.

I had wanted to do a law degree because I wanted to change the world. When I graduated from law school I worked in the Family Law Section of the Legal Aid Commission. As I was processing maintenance applications through the local court, I felt more like a cog in a wheel rather than working on the issues that I thought were pressing. I was feeling frustrated and I went and spoke to Roberta Sykes about the fact that I thought I would go back to do some more study and perhaps find work at the university. I had been teaching general studies classes — Aboriginal history, culture and contemporary issues — and I really enjoyed the experience. Education became an area that I saw as increasingly important if there were to be greater understanding in Australian society about Indigenous issues.

I spoke to Roberta about this and told her I thought I would like to do a Masters. She encouraged me, but added, "You should apply to Harvard". I didn't take it seriously because I thought Harvard was out of my league. When Roberta handed me the forms to fill in, I was too frightened of her to say "No", and so dutifully filled them in and sent them off. I never expected to get in and I couldn't have been more surprised when I eventually found myself on a plane to Boston. I was worried for the first few weeks that I would be told that there had been a mistake and I had not been accepted. In the years since I have often been asked how I got to Harvard, and I think that the expectation is that I will talk about goal-setting and ambition, but the truth is I never saw myself as having as much potential as Roberta thought I had. She was the best mentor that I could have ever had.

Harvard was an amazing time. Away from Australia, I was able to try things I didn't have time for at home. In addition to my regular studies I did courses in Spanish, French, creative writing and film. I also audited classes, including several Law and Literature classes, and a class taught by the great Spike Lee on African-American film. I started a writing group and a book club. The intellectual life was like nothing I had ever experienced. You could hear Noam Chomsky speak before heading off to a Russian Film Festival. People as diverse as the Dalai Lama, Yasser Arafat and Oliver Stone came to give lectures.

There were also many interesting Australians who travelled through at the same time that I was at Harvard. One of the highlights was meeting Justice Tony Fitzgerald, an Australian judge who had conducted the major inquiry into corruption in the Queensland Police Service. I had always admired him as someone who had a great legal mind and a social conscience. His judgements always remained faithful to the rule of law, but retained an eye on social justice, and I thought his legal style was something that I would like to emulate. He gave a speech at the Law School and I met him there. He and his wife were supportive of my efforts and he became one of my most active mentors after that meeting. I was so touched that someone like Justice Fitzgerald would take the time to ensure that whenever I asked for his advice he was available to give it. He launched my second book, *Achieving Social Justice*, which was based on my doctoral dissertation.

I came to do my doctorate at Harvard Law School in similar circum-stances to those that saw me enrol there in the first place. I was taking a class with Roberto Mangabiera Unger, who was one of the people who had led the Critical Legal Studies movement. He is one of the world's greatest legal theorists and I was completely intimidated by him. I decided to do my class assignment on the recognition of Aboriginal sovereignty in Australia, and when I asked Professor Unger about the issue he told me that it would make a good doctoral thesis. He asked me if I had applied to do the doctoral program at Harvard. I told him that I hadn't and he asked me why. I told him that I didn't think that I would get in. He looked at me as though I was a bit stupid, and I felt so embarrassed I applied. Just like with Roberta, I was lucky that Professor Unger thought more of my abili-ties than I did. If it hadn't have been for his encouragement I would never have thought I could do a doctorate at Harvard Law School.

Working with Professor Unger was an amazing experience. I remained intimidated by his intellect, but it made me all the more determined to work hard and be prepared for our meetings. He really made me do my best work and I learnt a great deal through complet-ing that thesis. Graduation was one of the proudest days of my life, and perhaps the first time I thought that maybe I wasn't so dumb after all. I wouldn't have got through the doctorate without a strong support network of friends and a loving partner and I really felt, when I graduated, that it had been a team effort.

After graduating I worked in Canada for a year for a number of Indigenous, or First Nations as they are called there, organisations that gave me great insights into comparative aspects of Aboriginal legal issues between Australia and Canada. When I came back to Australia I took a job that saw me returning to the tertiary sector. Although my primary job was at a university, I was still passionate about Aboriginal legal and policy issues and I became involved with lots of different community organisations and projects. One of those was Black Women's Action in Education Foundation which was an organisation that Roberta Sykes had started. It raises money for Aboriginal people who want to pursue their education, especially overseas. It had funded my air travel to and from Harvard and I was keen to provide others with the same opportunities that I had. I was also pleased to return to my network of friends. With the best friendships, time apart seems to not make any difference at all, and I was lucky to have a strong support to meet me when I returned.

I was overwhelmed at what opportunities my higher degrees opened up for me, and I grabbed every opportunity that came along that I thought was interesting. People would marvel at how hard I worked, but it never felt that way because I was always working on issues that I felt passionate about. It has been hard to learn to say "No" to all of those opportunities, but I eventually learnt the hard way after several bouts of ill-health because I was pushing myself too hard and not taking enough time to rest. This inability to juggle a professional and private life came at a high cost to my marriage. The other lesson I learnt was to make sure that I spend time nurturing the relationships that nurture me.

One of the best opportunities that came my way at this time was the director's position at the Jumbunna Indigenous House of Learning at the University of Technology, Sydney. This gave me a chance to work in a broad range of areas of Indigenous education — student support, academic programs, and research — with a vibrant and inspiring Aboriginal team. There are almost 30 people working at Jumbunna and most of them are Aboriginal or Torres Strait Islanders. We work in collaboration with several community organisations including, Boomali, the National Aboriginal and Islander Skills Development Association (NAISDA), and the Aboriginal Justice Advisory Council. One of my favourite parts of my job is working with graduate students who are on the same pathway as I was on. Watching students go through the process of doing a doctorate is something that I feel very honoured to participate in, and I am proud of each person who undertakes that great achievement. I have also enjoyed watching the research team that my colleague, Professor Martin Nakata, and I have developed at Jumbunna. To see a new generation of young intellectuals carving out careers for themselves is something that has given me a lot of satisfaction.

I have also tried to keep active with my legal interests, working in my chosen profession and developing my legal skills. I was appointed to the Administrative Decisions Tribunal in the Equal Opportunity Division, allowing me to deal with a broad range of matters under the NSW anti-discrimination legislation. Similarly, sitting on the Serious Offenders Review Council has meant that I have worked on issues related to the general prison population, and this has given me insights into the criminal justice and corrective services systems that have enabled me to develop my thinking on Indigenous legal issues.

When I began working in Aboriginal politics, I was shocked at the level of base sexism that I encountered, sometimes from men who I had long admired for their outspoken advocacy on Aboriginal rights. There were many occasions when I sat in meetings and began to more and more appreciate the hard, tiring work that women like Marcia Langton and Roberta Sykes have done to ensure that a new generation of women were able to come into rooms that were previously so male dominated. I felt their unacknowledged ground-breaking was something I was receiving the privilege of.

I also began to realise that I had been blessed with the advantage of knowing who I was and where I came from. Anyone who thinks that Aboriginal politics is welcoming and warm has not worked there. One of the cheapest shots that people make when they resent the presence of others is to question their Aboriginality. Coming from a family that was recognised and accepted as part of the Aboriginal community meant that I have never had to fear these kinds of demeaning remarks. But I have observed many Aboriginal people, especially young ones, who were adopted out or dislocated from their Aboriginal families who cannot make the same clear claims to family and country. There are people within the community who are quick to discredit others and undermine the confidence of those seeking to participate and speak out. I abhor this treatment. We, as Aboriginal people, have fought a long campaign to have the impact of the child removal policy recognised, remedied, and compensated. To turn on members of our own community who are living with the effects of those policies and who therefore cannot name their family is cruel. I have seen many young people struggle with this insecurity about their identity. It is soul-destroying to have members of the Aboriginal community attack them.

Have courage

People often ask me what my greatest achievement is. I would have to say that it would be a tie between supervising Indigenous doctoral students and writing. My first novel was published in 2004. I have always loved writing, but only resumed creative writing when I was in Boston with the encouragement of my close friends and the writing group we established. *Home* is a story about the impact of the removal policy on three generations of an Aboriginal family. It seeks to explore how pervasive the psychological impact was, and to show that Indigenous people and families still live with the effects of that policy today. It is a very personal story and I feel that there is an increasing need to continue to tell those stories, because I feel that we are living in an era in Australia that is becoming increasing disinterested in Indigenous issues.

I had always thought that if people knew the human cost of policies like the removal of children on Aboriginal people that there would be increased understanding as to why our communities and families face the issues that we do. I was shocked that some sectors of the Australian community responded to personal accounts from the stolen generations by attempting to deny their experience and trivialise their hurt and suffering. I felt it was really important to continue to tell those stories so they would not be marginalised or forgotten. Writing *Home* and getting it published was something I feel very proud of, and although it got mostly rave reviews, there was one that trashed it by saying that it was too political and not well edited. I was crushed at first, despite all the wonderful and positive things that were said about the novel. I made the mistake of listening to only the bad review, not all the good ones. But the more I thought about it I did feel proud that, even if there was a negative reaction, I had taken the brave step of putting out there a story I believe in. You can't expect to make a contribution to public life without taking criticism. But that doesn't mean that it is easy, and at these times, more than ever, that network of peer and mentor support is valuable beyond words.

Over the last decade of working on Indigenous issues, I have felt that attitudes have hardened towards Aboriginal and Torres Strait Islander people, and that there is less interest and sympathy than there was in the previous decade of reconciliation. As Australians become more focused on issues of national security, border protection, and interest rates, it has become a bigger challenge to draw attention to the pressing issues of Indigenous health, education, housing, culture, heritage, wellbeing, and self-determination. This is especially so with the current Howard Government focusing on remote areas, leaving the socio-economic needs of urban and rural Indigenous communities unmet.

One of the hardest personal challenges I have felt in my work is that there seems to have been little increase in interest and understanding of these complex Indigenous issues in urban areas. People see images of a riot in Redfern and are frightened. But they will not take the time to understand and address the complex range of social issues that lead to that sort of flashpoint so as to try and prevent a reoccurrence.

Many times in the last few years I have found strength in the words of Martin Luther King. He said that, in the end, we would remember the silence of our friends more than the words of our enemies. He also said that we begin to die the day we stop working for the things that matter. I find both of those sentiments inspiring.

There is another story that I also take encouragement from. It is about an old man on a beach that is covered in starfish that have been washed up from the sea. He is picking up the starfish and throwing them back into the water. A young man walks up to him and says that there are so many starfish that it would be impossible to save them all so his hard work is being wasted because it will make no difference. The old man replies simply, "It will make a difference to the starfish that I just threw back into the sea".

Gordon Samuels AC, CVO

by
Selina Samuels

Gordon J. Samuels was Governor of New South Wales from 1996 to 2001. He serves currently as a part-time Commissioner for the New South Wales Law Reform Commission, as the Chair of various legal committees, and in particular assisted in the conduct of an inquiry for the New South Wales Government into aspects of criminal law procedures. Previously he was Chancellor of the University of New South Wales, Chairman of the NSW Law Reform Commission, and a Judge of the NSW Supreme Court and of the Court of Appeal. His other roles included Chairman of the NSW Migrant Employment and Qualifications Board, Presiding Member of the Independent Advisory Committee on the Educational Needs of Overseas Trained Doctors, Chairman of the Australian Legal Education Council, and President of the Security Appeals.

Gordon Samuels' job titles over the years have included, barrister, Queen's Counsel, Judge of the NSW Supreme Court and Court of Appeal, Chancellor of the University of New South Wales, and Governor of New South Wales. He is clearly recognised and honoured as a notable and inspiring leader. He is also my father.

Therefore, to attempt any form of biography could be considered difficult. To claim that one can know one's subject or can represent that subject objectively and completely is multiplied the closer the biographer is to her subject. What becomes so problematic is disassociating the writer from the subject, the writer's bias from the portrait, the intimate knowing from the public knowing, and the things that one has always believed from what everyone else has always believed. So, if the family rather than the public man gets some attention, and if I creep in occasionally (with my mother and my sister), I hope that you will not be too alarmed, but will recognise — as I have had to recognise — that no biographer can hope to find a single subject, and that to represent any subject singly would be false.

Gordon Jacob Samuels was born on the 12th August, 1923 at home in Cricklewood, a suburb in north London, the only child of Harry Samuels and Zelda Selina Samuels (née Glass). My grandfather Harry was an Australian, born in Walcha on the New England tableland in New South Wales. He was the eldest of four sons of Jacob, a Jewish migrant from Vilna in Lithuania who had migrated to Scotland during the 1880s at a time when many Jewish migrants left Eastern Europe, although there is no clear evidence to suggest he was escaping from pogroms or other anti-semitic activities. There he met and fell in love with a young friend of the family, Mary Michaelson. Jacob left Mary behind when he moved to Australia a while later, but in 1887, after some family opposition, Mary followed him and they were married. Soon after they settled in Walcha in New South Wales and opened a store. Given the representations of the Australian bush during this period, made famous by writers such as Henry Lawson and Banjo Paterson, it is hard to believe that the Samuels family was so readily accepted by a small and unsophisticated rural community, but there is evidence to suggest that they assimilated not only into the rural Jewish community, but into the area in general. Jacob was elected Mayor in 1903 and there is a photograph of him in the local Council Chamber, something from which Gordon derives enormous delight.

When the World War I began Harry and Louis, the two eldest Samuels boys, enlisted for overseas service. Eddie, the youngest remaining son, was unfit for duty and served in the army in Australia. During leave Harry visited family in Newcastle-upon-Tyne, where he met his future wife. My grandmother, Zelda Selina or Selina Zelda Glass (she was known as Selina in Newcastle and Zelda in London), was born to migrants from Riga in Latvia and was brought up in a more or less orthodox Jewish household in Newcastle. Harry and Zelda were married in 1921 (he was 31, she was 23) and they went to live in London, where Harry established himself as a clock and watch importer. And so Gordon was born in an ordinary, middle-class garden suburb in the north-west of London.

Gordon's first school was a privately owned and run primary school which he attended from the age of five until six or seven, where he learnt — just — to read and possibly to write and to sew a canvas bag and a raffia mat, feats that impressed his father not at all. Harry was given to producing these objects at dinner parties and announcing that they had cost him seven guineas, or whatever the cost of school fees was. Gordon was then enrolled in a proper preparatory school, Sunbury House, again a private school, but with a decent academic reputation. There he met the headmaster, Pilliner, a man whom he has described as one of the most unforgettable characters he has ever met.

Pilliner's aim was to prepare boys for scholarships to enter secondary schools, and by all accounts he was remarkably good at it. In sixth-form, at the age of 12, Gordon was force-fed trigonometry, algebra and geometry, introduced to Trollope and Dickens, essay and letter writing. For punishment, the boys were tied to the ship's bell that marked the change of class. They were tied by the neck to the lanyard and had to stand on tip-toe to avoid clanging the bell, which would bring further punishment. It sounds terribly Dickensian, and even quite appalling by modern standards, but clearly Pilliner got results. Not only did he make a deep impression on Gordon — he introduced him to scholarship and discipline and to Dickens, one of his favourite authors (I think the trigonometry has made less of a lasting impression) — most of the sixth form got scholarships to the public schools of their choice. Pilliner was not completely without affection for the boys, however. Gordon is adamant that I mention that, although he hammered the boys in class and on the sports field, he also gave the sixth form wonderful treats. He took them to the Observatory and to the Royal Naval College at Greenwich, and to watch divers working in the River Thames. Then, after an outing, he would stand all eight or ten of them to a slap-up meal in the West End. Gordon's admiration for Pilliner is telling — it reveals his delight in the eccentric personality and his complete lack of resentment. Treatment that might have generated anxiety and self-pity (and certainly would have in a more contemporary context) merely focused Gordon's mind.

Gordon won a scholarship and went to University College School, which had the reputation of being modern with good academic standards. It was nearby in Hampstead and was founded on an ideology of tolerance. There was no corporal punishment — unusual for a school of that time. Gordon opted for History and English, Latin and Greek, and more or less abandoned maths and science after the School Certificate. He maintained his academic standards, inculcated by Pilliner, and worked towards university admission.

Although neither Harry or Zelda had gone to university, there was no question that Gordon would go, and certainly no question that he would aim for a history scholarship to Balliol College, Oxford. The emphasis on education in the Samuels family reveals a certain Jewish bias towards education even by those who were themselves poorly educated. Neither Harry nor Zelda were intellectuals, although both were reasonably well read and interested in music (Harry played the violin and Zelda the piano, which may explain Gordon's love of music), but there was a great emphasis placed on Gordon's intellectual development and never any suggestion that he would follow his father into the clock and watch business.

Gordon sat for his Higher Certificate in the summer of 1940, in the midst of the wartime air-raid blitz on London and south-east England. He had been prepared for the war. Both he and his father were sure that the war would break out, although Harry still travelled in Germany up until 1938 for business. In the buildup to war, Gordon and other boys from school joined the Air Raid Precautions (ARP) service, and went around fitting people with gas-masks. He was then switched to a Control Centre — "the Hub", which directed relief services like the ambulance, fire and rescue in the event of "an incident". He recalls walking home at lunchtime through the local park on the day war was declared, a sunny Sunday, and the park was full as usual, but everyone was carrying their gas masks.

The outbreak of war, not surprisingly, distracted him. Their home in Cricklewood was bombed and the family moved to St Albans, about 20 miles out of London. He had to travel into school and back again, studying in the midst of air-raids and continuing to work at the ARP, but he got his history scholarship to Balliol and went up in the summer term of 1941. He recalls that the essay question for the scholarship exam was on justice and he was able to preface his essay with the Latin quote "fiat justifier ruat coelum" (he has a ridiculously good memory for Latin).

Gordon had already enlisted in the army and would be called in about July 1942, allowing him to do only four terms at Oxford. This created a problem as four terms of history would not allow him to gain a degree, yet four terms of law would under a special war degree program. Law then became a much more profitable option. So, after consulting with the law don and his father, who said "give it a shot", and his great friend Louis Bielinky, who had picked him for a lawyer in the first place, he changed from history to law. From the moment of his decision, he never wavered in his attachment to law as a study and as a profession, and by summer 1942 he had his law degree. He revelled in the romance of studying in Oxford just prior to going to the war. His continued attachment to the poetry of A.E. Houseman is linked to this.

> Houseman wrote a book of poems called *A Shropshire Lad*, which was about Shropshire and about country people. It's full of poems of marvellous melancholy, and they're just the stuff to read to a girl in a punt, three weeks before leaving Oxford to go to the war.[1]

Gordon was posted to the Royal Artillery by dint of the training he had done in the Senior Training Corps at Oxford. He spent six months at the Officer Cadet Training Unit in Staffordshire, an experience that he characterises as great fun. His squad, largely made up of cynical intellectuals from Oxbridge who were known to their instructors as "the Bolshies", decided that their strength lay in unity and they would do all their exercise as a team, finishing together and resisting the urge for individual glory. I see this now as a strong

---

1 Gordon Samuels, Interview with Julia Horne, University Oral History Project of the UNSW Archives, 1996–1997.

theme in Gordon's life — a recognition of the benefits of team-work and the humbling of the self in favour of the group. He tells a particularly hilarious story about the last exercise of his battle-combat simulated training:

> ... we set off at dawn, went up into the mountains and then camped just at dusk. We cooked our meal and then we were awakened by people throwing thunder flashes around, which were dummy grenades. They make a hell of a noise and a big flash. So we had been attacked and we had to get home to our camp. We divided up into three sections of about 10 or so. We had a map, compass, off you go! The directing staff were patrolling the roads and therefore ensured that we went home across the mountains – in the dark ... So my section held a conference and we decided that it wasn't on to go home across the mountains. We knew there was a bus that ran to the village near where our camp was, and we knew that the staff were patrolling the road in trucks. What we did – and of course this was very good training actually – one after the other we shot like stones down the mountain side. We had to cross the road because the bus was going that way. One at a time doing what we'd been trained to do, we dashed across, hurled ourselves into the ditch on the other side. We got across without being detected. The bus came along and one stood up, bus stopped and we all piled on. The bus driver and the conductor were very co-operative. We lay on the floor of the bus. One or two passengers thought it was a great yell and the bus duly went into Penwyn Mawr. So we got out of the bus and there was a café. One at a time we dived through the door into the café. It was closed, about 10.30 at night, however, they opened up for us and we sat around there until we thought the fastest record-breaking squad might possibly have made it home across the mountain. So we muddied ourselves a bit more and we limped into camp, to be greeted with incredulity by the staff, who said it was a record, so we then went to bed. The next section came in about two hours later, and they had also decided that going across the mountain wasn't on. They thought the railway line was the thing. It's very difficult, though, because the railway sleepers aren't always a stride apart, so it's inconvenient, and then the tunnels were a bit dicey. Fortunately there were only one or two and they were quite short, but they'd got in one tunnel and heard a train coming so they all pressed against the wall. They got in, and at dawn the heroes arrived who actually had walked home across the mountains. It didn't take our directing staff long to work

out roughly what the story was. But they never said a word. They thought, rightly, that we'd shown considerable initiative. So it was great fun.[2]

At the age of 19, Gordon was commissioned as a Second Lieutenant (a promotion to Captain to come later) with the Royal Devon Yeomanry, a gunner regiment stationed, at the time of his commission, in Colchester, Essex. From there they went to Northern Ireland for training and where they were stationed. He has some funny stories to tell about Ireland, and negotiating, as a British officer, with the Irish for supplies and other important army matters. Perhaps, as a Jew, he was immune from the ramifications of the situation, although he was well aware of the tensions simmering under the surface. He would drink poteen with Mr Quinn, a publican from Cookstown who was also an IRA leader and would sell the regiment their liquor.

> I knew that he knew that I knew that he knew that I knew that if he met me on a dark night he would knock me on the head if he possibly could, and steal my revolver. But subject to that we were very good friends.[3]

In 1944 the regiment was posted to India to practice their assault on Malaya, which was planned as part of the Far East campaign. And in August 1945, just after the second bomb was dropped on Japan, they arrived in Malaya. What was planned as an offensive became a peace-keeping mission. My father has said from time to time that as horrific as the atomic bombs were, they probably saved his life and ensured mine. The British Army in Malaya had to disarm the Malay People's Anti-Japan Army, the communist guerrillas, who were posing a threat to civil order after the war, and kept peace between the Malays and Chinese. The legal structure in Malaya was in disarray and the regiment was ordered to supply two magistrates. One was a barrister and the other was Gordon — who, after four terms of law, could be said to have some kind of legal experience. He was 22 and had to make decisions with the help of interpreters because he was dealing with speakers of Malay, English, Tamil, Urdu and any number of Chinese dialects. He is conscious, in retelling this, of the extent to which it sounds almost offensively colonial — that as a British officer he felt he was naturally born to rule. But he learnt humility rather than arrogance from this experience, as well as quite a lot about Malaya, and, I think, about his own innocence. The experience in India and Malaya also taught him, or so he maintains, to tolerate very hot curries.

---

2 Gordon Samuels, Interview with Julia Horne, University Oral History Project of the UNSW Archives, 1996–1997.

3 Gordon Samuels, Interview with Julia Horne, University Oral History Project of the UNSW Archives, 1996–1997.

There is a contemporary temptation to attribute an enormous number of personal characteristics to the experience of war. For someone of my generation my father's recollections of war seem quaint and unreal — nothing at all like *M*A*S*H* or any of the other fictions we were exposed to as children. Gordon's insistence on the "fun" of his training seems to be a denial of the fear they must all have been feeling, the real dangers that they were anticipating. But he resists this reading, claiming that, unlike more recent wars such as Vietnam — which altered the public perception of war — WWII was viewed as a war that had to be fought, and good and evil were more clean-cut and identifiable. Even his friends who had been in combat were not particularly adversely affected in terms of psychological stress. And so, the war, more than anything else, was the beginning of years of leadership. Perhaps because he never saw combat his war experience seems to have been more about peace-keeping and justice than battle, and the legacy is similarly benign. The only damage he sustained from the experience was a burst eardrum (an unfortunate side-effect of the artillery), to which his family now attributes any deafness, vagueness, or lack of interest.

He was de-mobbed in early March 1946 and after reuniting with his mother (Harry had died in 1941) returned to Balliol to read for an honours degree in law. He recalls the years just after the war at Oxford with the glamorous patina of nostalgia. None of the returned officers seems ever to have done any work, and they spent a lot of time escaping in and out of Holywell Manor with the reluctant acquiescence of the Balliol Praefectus (a Balliol Fellow responsible for the Manor and welfare of graduates), who felt that he could not apply rules designed for undergraduates too stringently to veterans. My own momentary desire to do a PhD at Oxford (Balliol College, of course) was entirely fuelled by these memories, conveyed with my father's robust sense of humour with regard to youthful misdemeanors. I in fact eventually went to the University of London, and visiting friends in Oxford I was confronted with a sense that the whole university was still enmeshed in the romantic memories of my father, which no-one could ever truly recapture. Even I felt nostalgic about someone else's memories. Perhaps it hasn't really changed at all, but now the ritual is anachronistic and intellectual insouciance has been replaced by out-and-out competition (which was probably always there, just not in the stories I was told).

In 1947, Zelda — or Ma as she was known to my father and to many others — sold their house in London and set off by boat to Sydney, at the request of Harry's youngest brother Eddie (a pharmacist and amateur musical-comedy writer of considerable charm and some eccentricity). Gordon followed after being admitted to the Bar in London, and arrived in Australia in January 1949. The arrangement was that if he didn't like it, they'd both return to England. Yet Gordon already felt an emotional attachment to his new home. His father, after all, had been Australian. He also felt that his professional prospects would be better in the expanding economy of Australia than in an England that was still recovering from the battering of the war. He has always said that when he left London he left behind "my best girl, my best friend and my flat". Not that long after though his best friend married his best girl and went to live in Gordon's old flat. There was little to go back for.

Soon after arriving in Sydney, anxious to get a job and actually earn some money, Gordon went to work with a large firm of solicitors, Dawson Waldron Edwards & Nicholls (now Blake Dawson Waldron). This gave him the necessary experience and entrée into the profession, and three years later he went to the Bar. Again, just like Gordon's war recollections, this was all "great fun", and he recalls with affection some of his dodgier clients and more dubious winning arguments. His main work was insurance, defamation, and general commercial work. To supplement his practice he was also appointed Julius Stone's teaching fellow at Sydney University, teaching jurisprudence, and he has very fond memories both of Professor Stone and of academic teaching. Of course, if he had never done law but had stuck to history he would probably have been an academic, so being able both to practice law and to teach it was an ideal situation for him. Later, he was appointed the Challis Lecturer in Pleading at Sydney University, and lectured for six years in pleading, sometimes to as many as 180 students, half of whom had to sit in an adjacent room and watch him on closed-circuit television. His wife, the actor Jacqueline (Jackie) Kott, had to advise him not to wear stripes as these would disrupt the television picture.

Gordon took silk in 1964 and his practice continued to thrive. He cites one of the most important roles he ever performed as President of the Bar, a position to which he was elected in 1971. He took great pride in leading 400 members of his profession, and in this it is easy to see much the same factors operating as motivated him during the war — the importance of the team and both the pleasure of leading it and the responsibility of that position. "It was splendid", he says, "because I was representing my profession and representing something in which I believed". As President of the Bar he was involved, with Hal Wootton — founding Dean of the Law School of the University of New South Wales — in establishing the Aboriginal Legal Service, which enlisted the assistance of various law firms and barristers, and began to try and control and moderate police treatment of Aboriginals in Redfern. He appeared for a number of Aboriginal clients as well as a group of students who desegregated the cinema in Walgett. This experience is, once again, recounted as being "great fun". It is interesting to listen to Gordon's recounting of his involvement in something like the Aboriginal Legal Service; there is a careful disavowal of both ego and altruism. He would have you believe that he was involved because it was fun and for no other reason, and yet to do good has always been of utmost importance to him.

I asked Gordon what his colleagues would say of him as a lawyer: "I don't think anyone would say that I was the greatest lawyer of my generation. But they would say that I was the most persuasive advocate."

He was a great jury lawyer, and dealt as much, if not more, with factual disputes as legal ones, requiring a logical mind and careful consideration of detail. His wife, Jackie, maintains that his greatest asset as a lawyer, and indeed in everything he has done, has been a well-furnished mind and, I would add, considerable charm. These characteristics certainly recommended him to his profession when they elected him as President of the Bar, and were great assets to him as a judge.

In 1972 Gordon was recruited, along with his close friend Harold Glass, by the recently appointed Chief Justice of NSW, John Kerr. Although his practice was flourishing (or perhaps precisely because his practice was flourishing and he was consequently extraordinarily busy) Gordon was tempted by the offer to join the Bench. Although he was young for the appointment, 49, and although it meant a drop in income, he was attracted to the idea that he would have more time with his family (his first daughter, Deborah, was 10 and I was only four), and by the suggestion that he could contribute importantly to the court and to the administration of law. It is as a judge that I best remember him, and I think that despite the fact that he has a more romantic attitude to his time at the Bar, he is a natural judge — a problem solver, interested in finding truth above and beyond competition. He has said, "It was just a process of finding the answer, which was much more fun than presenting one part of the answer".[4]

In August 1974 he was appointed to the NSW Court of Appeal under the presidency of Athol Moffitt. He describes his role in the court as that of the "honest broker", the confidant of all the judges, and close to them all. He was also the editor, who would point out areas where judgments should perhaps be altered for sense or delicacy, a tendency he has not relinquished. Frank Hutley, a member of the court in the early days of Gordon's appointment and a great friend, said of his editorial tendencies: "If someone of the intelligence of Gordon can't understand it, then I'd better change it." He was more politically liberal than many of the other judges on the court, particularly in the earlier days, and would have enjoyed that as well. And, again, he remembers the experience of working in a team with great affection and, I think, pride.

---

4 Gordon Samuels, Interview with Julia Horne, University Oral History Project of the UNSW Archives, 1996–1997.

During the 20 or so years he served as a Supreme Court judge, Gordon began to be increasingly interested in law reform, particularly reform of the adversarial system. Despite his slightly romantic view of the practice of the law, and of course the "fun" of the Bar, he is not a traditionalist, and has always described his role as President of the NSW Law Reform Commission as one of his most satisfying and rewarding jobs. Rather than maintain the pure adversarial structure of the Westminster legal system, with the costs and delays of extensive document discovery and the ideology of winning obscuring the interests of finding the truth, he would advocate an incorporation of the inquisitorial procedures of the Continental legal system. In such a model the lawyers would assist the court — run by a judge with more power over the gathering of information and the pursuit of truth than the "referee" of the Westminster system — and the main aim would not be winning in the manner of a sporting competition (it has often been suggested that the model for the Westminster system is cricket), but the discovery of the facts and the truth. He is a staunch believer in the law, who wants it to work as efficiently and as effectively as possible. The willingness to accept change and, indeed, to initiate it, is one of Gordon Samuels' most marked leadership qualities.

In the midst of his judicial duties, Gordon was appointed the Chancellor of the University of New South Wales in 1976. He had been appointed to the University Council in 1969, when the Bar was asked to provide a representative to the Council. Gordon had always been interested in universities, and was interested in being involved in the development of a new university (it was known as the University of Technology from 1949 until 1958, and was then renamed the University of New South Wales). He describes the young university as: "hungry; it was the epitome of the hungry fighter seeking success and recognition."[5] Gordon felt strongly the desire to participate in this fight — primarily against the condescension of Sydney University — and although the role of Chancellor is honorary and therefore an unpaid position, he set out to be far more than a distant dignitary. As Patrick O'Farrell describes him in his history of the university: "A man of extraordinary energy and broadness of interest — was it boring being a justice of the Supreme Court? — Samuels very actively involved himself in university affairs. No more shaker of graduate hands at degree conferring ceremonies (though he was that, too), he was much taken up with the matters of high university policy: appointments, reputation, power plays, on most of which he had strong and interventionist opinions. A similarly striking personality was his wife, the actress Jacqueline Kott. They made a formidable pair, with no bones about asserting their pre-eminent role."[6]

---

5 Gordon Samuels, Foreword, *UNSW: A Portrait*, Patrick O'Farrell, Sydney: UNSW Press, 1999, p. 1.

Gordon saw the role of Chancellor to "act as honest broker within the university; and to act as the sounding-board for my vice-chancellor. In order to perform the second role, one had to know a good deal about what went on in the university".[7] His knowledge of the workings of the university, and his recognition of those people who actively participated in developing the institution, made him (and Jackie, who worked tirelessly for the university: sorting books for the Book Fair, running Kensington Lectures, leading the clapping at graduations and discussing university politics endlessly) enormously popular with and trusted by the academic staff. Past Vice-Chancellor, Professor John Niland, described him in glowing terms when he was appointed as Governor: "He has a deep interest in fairness, a steadying influence where emotions sometimes run deep, plays the figurehead role well, has an eloquence beyond words, an ear for all viewpoints and a very strong streak of independence."[8] Gordon was even quite popular with the students. I remember some years ago (I was still at school) a group of students from the council 'kidnapped' Gordon and forced him, at cap-gun point, to drive them to his chambers, firing their cap-guns all the way. The whole event was conducted with some hilarity. He was mostly concerned that they would get into all sorts of trouble with the security within the court. Despite his admonitions, and the coffee and tea his tremendous and long-suffering Associate, Margaret Anderson (who is still his secretary), served them, one did get away and held up a judge on another floor, who didn't have a sense of humour. When contacted by phone Jackie refused to pay any ransom, so the Vice-Chancellor of the time, Professor Michael Birt, was forced to negotiate.

Gordon's involvement in the workings of the university was considerable. He was the patron of nearly every sporting club in the university (and a founder of the Chancellor's cricket team). He was actively involved in the development and patronage of the Australia Ensemble, originally the University of New South Wales Ensemble. He chaired inquiries into conduct at a number of the resident colleges of the university and was involved — officially or unofficially — with many controversies that took place on the campus, and which provided rich fodder for dinner-table discussions.

Most controversial of all, he lead the strong opposition within the university of the proposed reforms to the university structure, presented by the New South Wales Government in 1988, and generally known as "Amalgamation". In the same year the Dawkins White Paper

---

6 Patrick O'Farrell, UNSW: A Portrait, p. 183

7 Gordon Samuels, Interview with Julia Horne, University Oral History Project of the UNSW Archives, 1996–1997.

8 Quoted by Tony Stephens, "A well-cast pragmatist", The Sydney Morning Herald, 20 January 1996.

on Tertiary Education abolished the division between colleges of advanced education (CsAE) and universities. The NSW Minister for Education, Dr Terry Metherell, then announced a plan to amalgamate UNSW and four country CsAE. These five institutions or campuses would then have become a mega University of New South Wales. Each would have had a small governing body responsible only for the domestic affairs of the campus; and there would have been an umbrella council responsible for the government of the whole five-campus university. This would, of course, have meant the dissolution of the existing Council of UNSW and its replacement by a small body with domestic responsibilities. This was considered by Gordon, and the majority of the university community, as an insupportable suggestion that would not only erode the standards of the university, but would also be an administrative nightmare. He feared that the life and the future of UNSW, by then a fast-expanding institution with a growing reputation, would have been assigned to a council of most uncertain composition and inadequate numbers. Gordon entered into the fray, and was considered then, as much as in hindsight, the commander of the battle. I remember attending a lunchtime meeting in the Clancy Auditorium at the university (I was then a student) opposing amalgamation, where he gave a most rousing speech denouncing the proposal and moving everyone to resist. There was, and still is, great affection among the academic staff for what they saw as action that protected their university. The resistance was successful. Amalgamation did not take place. There was, however, a change to the constitution of the size of the university council, which was reduced in size in order to follow the model of corporate boards. Despite the suggestion by O'Farrell that Gordon may have been moved by a fear of the "diminution of personal chancellorial power",[9] he also comments on his attitude to the Council and the university, "not as efficient corporate entities, but as voices, talking-shops, forums for discussion and debate."[10] As Gordon himself has said: "I've always taken the view that the university council is not merely for decision-making, it is also a wailing wall. Its purpose is to provide a forum for people in the university, elected by sectors in the University, to express apprehensions, complaints, criticism and to talk."[11] Again, he places an emphasis on the team, on mutuality and discussion and negotiation; a leader, certainly, but a leader who is also part of the group and wants, above all, to maintain that cohesion and the strength it confers. Both he and the university also recognised the incomparable contribution paid by Jackie — the "Samuels" building was named for both of them.

---

9 Patrick O'Farrell, *UNSW: A Portrait*, p. 239.

10 Patrick O'Farrell, *UNSW: A Portrait*, p. 238.

11 Gordon Samuels, Interview with Julia Horne, University Oral History Project of the UNSW Archives, 1996–1997.

After 18 years in the role of chancellor, Gordon retired from the university in 1994. He had already retired from the Bench, was the chairman of the Law Reform Commission of New South Wales, and wanted to do something else. He established himself as an Arbitrator and Mediator, and did a number of inquiries, including the 1993 inquiry into the dismissal of Pickard as the Agent-General for New South Wales in London. In 1994 Gareth Evans, then the Minister for Foreign Affairs, asked Gordon to head an inquiry into the Australian Secret Intelligence service (ASIS). A couple of former ASIS officers had been interviewed on *Four Corners* on the ABC, without divulging their identities, and had made a number of allegations about the inefficiencies of the organisation and the oppressive and unfair way it treated its officers. The inquiry was set up, in the words of Senator Evans, to focus on the "control and accountability" of ASIS and the "organisation and management of the service".[12] Not surprisingly, the Samuels Inquiry attracted considerable media attention — it was, as Gordon has pointed out, a bit like a John Le Carré novel — and it was unprecedented in the world of spying. According to an article by Philip Knightley in *The Australian,* the British Secret Service was so worried about the ramifications of the decision that it dispatched "a senior officer to Australia to advise ASIS on how to react".[13] It was a big job, requiring constant travel to Canberra and vigilant secrecy. Gordon enjoyed it. Not only was it fascinating material, but he was pleased with the team he had around him. I remember that he was particularly amused by the younger staff members who were initially baffled by his sense of humour, but became so fond of him that they provided not one but two birthday cakes for the office celebration.

In the end his judgment ruffled some feathers, although only the sanitised version was published and the final report is still top secret. He found that while the more extravagant allegations were unproven, there was still cause to criticise ASIS's organisation and make some recommendations about reform. In general the media and most commentators depicted Gordon Samuels as incorruptible (a particularly relevant issue in a spy inquiry) and independent, and there was little criticism of the judgment by the press.

The media interest in the ASIS inquiry, however, was nothing to the attention they focused on the announcement that Gordon Samuels was to be the next Governor of New South Wales. Bob Carr, Premier of NSW, first spoke to Gordon about the position in 1995, and after careful consideration and much discussion with Jackie (and some discussion with Deborah and myself) he decided to accept the position, and it was announced to the public in January 1996. The

---

12 Cameron Stewart, "ASIS probe will study control, not role", *The Australian*, 1 March 1994.

13 Philip Knightley, "Self-Service", *The Australian*, 20 February 1995.

terms of the position were that they would not live in Government House, and that the ceremonial trimmings would be reduced. And so the press coined the phrase "no frills Governor" and "part-time Governor". In addition, he was the first Jewish Governor, probably the first migrant Governor (leaving aside Governors before 1946, who had all been British), and the first lawyer.

There was much confusion, of course. Many people were outraged that the Premier had rudely kicked the Governor out of Government House. Although it was the decision of the Premier initially, both Gordon and Jackie were considerably relieved that they did not have to leave their newly renovated home in Bronte and move into an imposing sandstone edifice. The "Part-Time Governor" tag originated from Gordon's initial desire to maintain his position as chair of the NSW Law Reform Commission, and reduce some of his ceremonial responsibilities to allow him to do so. It was never suggested that his constitutional responsibilities would be altered in any way, and fairly soon it became clear that he would not be able to continue with the Law Reform Commission and he resigned before becoming Governor.

There were people who approached Gordon and Jackie at dinner parties to say how terrible it was that the Governor and his wife did not reside where they should, in Government House. There was anxiety about the constitutional ramifications of the reforms to the position, anxiety that was completely unfounded, but born, perhaps, of distrust of the role of politicians in the process. Re-reading the newspaper reports dealing with the issue, it is surprising that other-wise fairly rational reporters responded so negatively to the reform of the role — minor though it was. But there was also a great deal of support and affection for the Governor-delegate and his wife, and some lovely cartoons parodying the idea of a "suburban" governor, with the Queen and Prince Philip being directed to "Gordon's" house by a local yobbo, or the Queen sitting up to breakfast at the kitchen bench, served by the Governor and his wife in their dressing gowns. The press overran the Bronte house, which had just been finished and still had no garden, and there are lots of juxtaposed photographs of the grand facade of Government House with the "modest" house in Bronte, surrounded by post-renovation rubble and dirt. The press were very respectful, however, and went away when asked to. The media were particularly taken with Jackie, who is always described in the articles in the most glowing terms: as Gordon's "extremely able and attractive wife"[14] with "the elegance and melodious voice of her long acting career".[15] Many of the press reports consistently refer to her as Ms Kott in deference to her independence. Ultimately, the charm of both Governor-delegate and

Governor's wife won over the public and the press, with reports describing their "genuine graciousness" and "common-touch humanity".[16] Gordon's comment — that after a lifetime of dressing up, as barrister, judge, Chancellor and now Governor — he would call his biography *My Life in Drag* was met with much more hilarity than shock, and it was suggested to me by some of my gay friends — with considerable respect and enthusiasm — that he should have a mayoral float at the next Gay and Lesbian Mardi Gras Parade.

In Gordon's swearing-in speech he stressed the importance of the role of Governor of NSW in the encouragement of understanding between all groups of the community — Aboriginals, migrants and other minority and marginalised groups. He also recognised the importance of recognising volunteers and others whose work in the community is so valuable although monetarily unrewarded. he sees the many country visits that the he and Jackie have undertaken are vital to recognise and honour the country regions, which tend to be ignored in favour of the larger centres. Gordon and Jackie are particularly impressed by the pride people take in their towns, their regions, and by their delight that the Governor and his wife should visit. And people are pleased that Gordon and Jackie are so ordinary — staying in the local motel and driving a Ford LTD (although most children, when asked to draw the Governor and his wife preparatory to their visit, depict them in crowns and ermine, driving a horse-drawn carriage).

Again, Gordon's role was defined by a sense of mutuality, of community. He led by example, but also by encouragement and hard work. His partnership with Jackie is of central importance in this position, as it has been important throughout his career. They are very much a team, a fact that was recognised in many of the early press reports. Both of them are, at heart, performers, and both have a strong sense of the need for the recognition and reward of those who work tirelessly and selflessly for the good of the community.

My father met my mother, Jacqueline Kott, in 1956. She is an actor, and had just returned from five years working in repertory theatre in the UK. Her father, a solicitor in Perth, had sent her a return ticket in 1955. She wouldn't accept a single ticket as she was determined to return to England. Soon after she was offered a job with an English tour with Sybil Thorndike, Lewis Casson, Ralph Richardson and Meriel Forbes. They play came on tour to Sydney and my parents met at a party held by the barrister Tom Hughes and his first wife, Joanna, in their flat at Manar in King's Cross. Joanna had intended to act as matchmaker, but this was redundant. Gordon walked into the room,

14 Sir Asher Joel, "Governors I have known", *The Sydney Morning Herald*, 20 January 1996.

15 Leonie Lamont, "We could put up the Queen, at a pinch", *The Sydney Morning Herald*, 18 January 1996.

16 "The right couple for the job", *The Daily Telegraph*, 20 January 1996.

saw a girl in a blue dress talking to one of his students from the Law School (where he was at the time teaching part-time) and immediately exerted the tutor's right and sent him on his way. I remember being told as a child that they fell in love at first sight and later that night, having supper together, may father was so overcome with love that he cut a plate in half and bit a chunk out of a glass. It was years before I considered that alcohol might have been slightly more to blame. Not long after they met Jackie went on tour around NSW with *The Summer of the Seventeenth Doll,* during which Gordon thought hard about what he should do. On her return he proposed. According to Gordon, Jackie immediately said, "Yes". She maintains that she paused for at least a couple of seconds between question and answer. They married a year later, on 4 April 1957.

Zelda wasn't completely thrilled by the match. Not only was Gordon her only child and relative in Sydney, he was "marrying out" (although Max, my grandfather, was Jewish, Lillian, Jackie's mother, was not). Apparently, at one point she told Gordon to choose between his mother and his fiancée, which he pretty much ignored. From what I can gather Ma and Jackie — both strong-willed and determined women — were never completely reconciled until just before Ma's death from renal failure (before either my sister or myself were born), when Ma had to confess that she couldn't have imagined Gordon with anyone else. Max, on the other hand, was delighted with his new son-in-law, who was a lawyer and a Jew and not averse to a whisky or a glass of wine.

So, Jackie did not end up using the return ticket and did not return to England. She continued to work throughout the marriage — which was not a particularly common thing to do at the time. It is hard to say if her career suffered from her marriage. Certainly, the wife of a successful barrister can be subsumed into the life of the law, and she did not, perhaps, maintain the kind of connection with the theatrical world that she might have had she married someone else. As a child my consciousness of her profession was, however, stronger than my understanding of my father's. Actors are a little more glamorous than lawyers, after all, even if dressing up is required in both professions. But from my standpoint now I can see how much she gave up for my father; not necessarily rejecting parts or tours — we managed very well on the number of occasions we were left to fend for ourselves — but in becoming a lawyer's wife rather than exclusively an actor. Perhaps, as well, she was attracted to the professional world that my father inhabited, particularly to the world of the university where they increasingly spent so much time. My mother, like my father, is essentially an intellectual.

In preparing this essay, I asked my father the questions he asks himself when he has to make a difficult decision. His first answer was, "How could I explain my decision to Jackie?" My mother has kept him honest, not because he has any real inclination towards dishonesty, but because, after arguing with her about something, it is more clearly defined in his mind. They talk about everything. As a young adult, when I still lived at home, I would go out to visit a friend after dinner, leaving my parents sitting at the dinner table, drinking wine and in the midst of an intense discussion (usually, during that period, about the university). I would return hours later to find them still sitting there, still discussing the same issue, although perhaps another bottle of wine would have been opened. Theirs is not the painful kind of marriage that one so often witnesses in restaurants, with a couple consuming their meal in complete silence. Silence has never been a particularly marked feature of the Samuels family.

After some anxiety that my mother would not be able to conceive, my sister Deborah was born in 1962, almost six years after my parents were married. I followed six years later, in 1968. My father maintains he never had any yearning for a son, and was completely satisfied by daughters who did not have to be taken to play football on Saturday mornings. He used to take us to ballet and sit quietly reading the paper while we trotted about in our leotards, convincing no-one that we were particularly gifted or graceful. After a fairly exclusive relationship with his mother, particularly in adulthood, I think he has always been extremely happy surrounded by women ("a monstrous regiment of women" as he would say), and does not have the tendency to patronise or condescend that other female-focused men of his generation often have. I remember when I was very young and thought that women were either secretaries or schoolteachers, that he explained to me patiently that women could do absolutely anything that they wanted. I think I was a little ashamed, even then, of my lack of imagination.

My father has had an enormous influence on my own scholarship and academic achievement. He sent me off to my first scholarship exams when I was in primary school with the pen and pencil he had been given for his Bar Mitzvah and told me, "The day of the exam always arrives, but it always passes" — a piece of remarkably sage advice that made me feel a whole lot better. He encouraged my intellectual curiosity by always providing an enormous number of resources in answer to every question and by encouraging me to read. It must have been the influence of Pilliner — I was presented with Dickens at an early age (I enjoyed **Nicholas Nickleby** in particular, I remember) and Trollope slightly later. We even read the Bible together in the evenings, an ideal background for an English academic, and very useful when teaching T.S. Eliot or Donne. Some years ago, when I was still living at home, my parents returned from a wedding anniversary party, during which all the children of the couple stood up and declared what their parents had taught them. My father, naturally, asked me the same question and all I could think of (I had just returned from a 21st birthday party and so was perhaps a bit the worse for wear) was "Read the Question".

At university, I began to get a clearer image of the regard in which my father is held by the rest of the world. I was a student in the Law School at the University of NSW, and so was fairly readily identifiable as my father's daughter. My lecturers spoke highly of him (and my colleagues in the school of English still do), and the students were all impressed rather than disparaging of my parentage. Even the student politicians and activists with whom I was friendly stopped short of denouncing the Chancellor — in deference, not to me, but to him. His interest in judicial reform inspired my interest in jurisprudence and legal philosophy. Although he was never convinced by my more extreme feminist jurisprudential arguments, he was completely supportive when, for a university assignment, I set off to interview female judges in NSW and put to them the need for feminist judging. He was considerably less conservative than most of them, I was happy to observe.

Most influential of all has been my father's careful and measured assessment of situations and arguments, without any party political interests whatsoever, or loyalties to any particular schools of thought. He considers matters entirely on their own merits, and gets to the heart of a problem, striving for a solution that is fair and just and appropriate. These judgments — personal as well as professional — are informed by a philosophy of compassion and tolerance and, of course, a strong sense of the law. A determination to judge every case on its merits enables him to stand outside political infighting. I find this so particularly in his clear discussion of legal issues that come up for political debate in the media. He is able to cut through the rhetoric and get to the point. I always find the clarity of my interpretation of any event considerably enhanced by a discussion with my father, and I know he was valued in the court, and at the university, as a wise arbiter and mediator.

Writing this account of my father's life, I have been surprised by some of the most salient points to emerge. I have tended to believe a feminist model of the genders, in which women's lives are constructed as based on community and interdependence, while men are considered to be more interested in autonomy, independence, and personal achievement and glory. But in recounting my father's life, I see his joy has been in being part of (perhaps leading, but nevertheless part of) the group — being at Oxford among other scholars, the pleasure of being part of the Bar, being a member of an appellate court, which naturally requires teamwork, being part of the university council and governing body, and his involvement with the community in his capacity as Governor of NSW. Even his stories about the war focus on the "fun" enjoyed by the group. This emphasis on community and no mutuality is a strong part of his sense of integrity. On my 18 birthday he wrote me a card in which he urged me to "do a little good for the world", and it is vital to any under-standing of his leadership qualities that he genuinely strives to contribute to the greater good, although without sentimentality or mawkishness, and with a sense of humour about the "worthiness" of such a stance. He is not without ego, by any means, but for a man like my father, doing good and gaining the recognition for doing good are in a fairly easy partnership.

I was in London when my father was sworn-in as Governor, and I was surprised when I received the photographs and noticed that he had donned a yarmulke as he took the solemn oath. I had seen him in his yarmulke before, of course, and I even recognised it as one that had belonged to his close friend Harold Glass, but I identified wearing it as a mark of religious affiliation and affirmation. My father is a Jew, but not a religious man by any means. Although he grew up in a Jewish household, he describes it as "compromise kosher"; they observed major festivals, shabbat and kiddush, changed dishes at Pesach and he took his Bar Mitzvah seriously, but they were not strictly orthodox. Then, at about the age of 14 he suddenly realised that religion seemed fairly irrational, and he instantly lost his faith and never regained it. Many of his contemporaries came to much the same conclusion at the same time, so it was not a terrible loss, and although his mother was a little disappointed (his father was relieved), it was much more convenient for playing cricket and football not to have to go to synagogue on Saturday morning.

Despite his lack of religion, he says he has a strong "atavistic feeling for Jewishness, which has grown, naturally, as a result of the Holocaust", and felt the need, when assuming the office of Governor, to represent himself as part of the community. He felt he should "publicly recognise that I am a Jew". My surprise at this was mingled with a sense of relief, because although we have not often discussed it, I feel very much the same way about being a secular Jew, even if so few people understand what it means, and I am sometimes made to feel that I am adopting an inauthentic identity, one which I have not earnt. The secular Jewishness of my father is a sense of identity that I have inherited inadvertently, because being Jewish was not a primary importance while I was growing up. By acknowledging, in a position of leadership, his identity as a secular Jew he was recognis-ing his heritage and his role within a community of which he cannot help but be a part.

I have had various images in mind — and, indeed, in front of me — while I have been writing this study of my father. There is a photo-graph of him just after the war. He is on a skiing holiday in Switzerland and looks quite ridiculously youthful and untouched to be a veteran of a war and a stint as magistrate in Malaya! There is a photograph of my parents cutting their wedding cake. They look like movie stars (I guess all children think their parents look like movie stars). And there is the portrait that Clifton Pugh painted of my father as Chancellor of the University of New South Wales. This was a controversial painting. Many people within the university disliked it intensely because it wasn't conventional, it didn't carry the weight of gravitas that they expected in an official portrait. But it is a wonderful representation of the man: Pugh has captured his humour and his cynicism, the look on his face when he is prepared to be convinced, but he knows that you will have to do a pretty good job. The portrait conveys intelligence and honesty, and it is an entirely accurate, and indeed insightful, representation of Gordon Samuels, lawyer, Chancellor and public man, and my father.

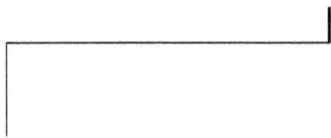

www.ingramcontent.com/pod-product-compliance
Lightning Source LLC
Chambersburg PA
CBHW070052120426
42742CB00048B/2501